NATION-BUILDING IN INDIAN ANTHROPOLOGY

Nation-Building in Indian Anthropology

Beyond the Colonial Encounter

ABHIJIT GUHA

MANOHAR
2022

First published 2022

ISBN 978-93-91928-73-5

Published by
Ajay Kumar Jain *for*
Manohar Publishers & Distributors
4753/23 Ansari Road, Daryaganj
New Delhi 110 002

Typeset by
Kohli Print
Delhi 110 051

Printed at
Replika Press Pvt. Ltd.

Dedicated to
Raghabendra Guha my uncle (Chotokaku)
whose invaluable collection of old books
in Anthropology was my first inspiration

Contents

Acknowledgements

The research for writing this book was made possible through a senior fellowship awarded to me by the Indian Council of Social Science Research (ICSSR), New Delhi, during 2018-20. I am indebted to the ICSSR for providing me financial support to carry out the aforementioned research on the 'Nationalist Trends in Indian Anthropology: An Historical Exploration'. I owe my debts to Institute of Development Studies Kolkata (IDSK), with which I was attached during the ICSSR senior fellowship period and its director, Professor Achin Chakrabarty, for providing me the infrastructural support to work on my research project. I am indebted to all the library staff at IDSK and, particularly, Sanjoy Kar, library assistant, for untiringly providing me with valuable articles. I am grateful to late Professor Vinay Kumar Srivastava, director, Anthropological Survey of India (AnSI), Dr Sasikumar Mundayat, deputy director of AnSI, and Dr Umesh Kumar, head of office, AnSI, Kolkata, for allowing me to use the central library of the institute. I am particularly indebted to Ramu Ram, librarian, and all the staff of the AnSI library who supplied me with the books and journals useful for my research. I owe my debt to my student, Subhra Bhattacharya, and her colleagues at the physical anthropology laboratory of AnSI who indefatigably supplied me with the hard and soft copies of the journal articles and books on my research topic. I am also grateful to Dr Nabakumar Duary for providing me with some of the valuable articles which I have used in this research. Dr Bidhan Kanti Das, Dr Gorky Chakrabarty, Smt Srija Mondal, Dr Subhanil Choudhury, Dr Ratna Dhar, Professor Kaushik Bose, Dr Subhamay Kisku, Dr Amit Kisku, Dr Uttam Bhattacharya, Dr Sumahan Bandopadhyay, Professor Dipak Midya, Dr Gautam Bera and Mr Tamil Selvan gave me immense intellectual inspiration to work on the history of anthropology in India. I am grateful to Manohar Publishers & Distributors and also to the anonymous reviewers without whose useful comments the book would not have been published. Last but not the least, I owe a lot to my wife, Priti, and younger son, Asi, who always showed enough patience to listen to my plans and progress on this research.

Medinipur
6 March 2021

ABHIJIT GUHA

CHAPTER 1

Introduction

History of Indian Anthropology as Depicted by the Founders

I

Anthropology in India began under colonial rule. The European scholars and British administrators contributed to the establishment of anthropology in India. The first anthropological publications started with the Asiatic Society, which was established on 15 January 1784 in Kolkata by Sir William Jones (1746-1794), a philologist. Although anthropology was not separately studied in this pioneering centre of learning in India, the scholars in Asiatic Society studied language, history, arts and the sciences. The *Memorandum of Articles* of the Asiatic Society, prepared by Jones read as follows:

> The bounds of investigations will be the geographical limits of Asia, and within these limits, its enquiries will be extended to whatever is performed by man or produced by nature (http://en.wikipedia.org/wiki/The_Asiatic_Society accessed on 8 February 2021).

The next impetus for anthropology in India came with the census operations by the British administration in 1881. Indian census data and its publications included a huge amount of anthropological information and the first census commissioner, Sir H.H. Risley (1851-1911), constructed the first racial classification of the Indian population. Censuses yielded massive biological and cultural information on the tribes and castes of India, which formed a major source of anthropological data. In a recent article A.C. Sinha has shown how anthropological methods were used by the British administration to collect census data for the colonial interests (Sinha 2021: 76-91). The first department of anthropology was established at Calcutta University in 1920 by the famous Indian vice-chancellor, Sir Asutosh Mukhopadhyay (1864-1924), and Ananthakrishna (1861-1937) (a pioneering Indian anthropologist) acted as its head. Famous Indian anthropologists, mostly trained outside India, were the founder teachers in the Department. Saratchandra Mitra (1863-1938), Ramaprasad Chanda (1873-1942), Haran Chandra Chakladar (1874-1958), Panchanan Mitra (1892-1936), B.S. Guha (1894-1961), K.P. Chattopadhyay (1897-1963), T.C. Das (1898-1964), N.K. Bose (1901-1972), D. Sen (1909-1980), S.S. Sarkar (1908-1969), and many others developed a strong empirical tradition of anthropology in India characterized by fieldwork in social-cultural anthropology and anthropometry in physical anthropology. The thrust on a holistic approach was the cardinal feature of anthropology in India. In contrast to Europe, Indian anthropologists paid more importance to the collection of data from the field rather than on building theories.

Gradually, universities in Lucknow, Delhi, Madras and Pune also developed strong traditions of anthropological research and teaching, and the largest governmental organization, the Anthropological Survey of India, was established by Dr B.S. Guha in 1946, which also began with the holistic framework of anthropology and added interdisciplinary collaborations with other biological and social sciences, like biochemistry, geography and linguistics.

Much later, and particularly after the independence of the country, Indian anthropologists felt that anthropology in India still remained a Western imitation, save some brilliant exceptional studies done by some of the pioneers. The crisis of Indian anthropology was also perceived at the level of application of anthropology for human welfare, national planning and national integration. Some of the anthropologists also ventured into the future of Indian anthropology. It is with the help of this background that I have written this book based on my research on the nationalist trends in Indian anthropology. This does not mean that Western traditions of Anthropology

(British, American or other foreign schools) were not followed by the nationalist anthropologists in India, nor do I mean that Indian problems around nation-building were not studied by the Western anthropologists. Very recently, three leading British universities (Leeds, Edinburgh and Manchester) have undertaken a mega research project in 2019 entitled 'The Other from Within: Indian Anthropologists and the Birth of the Nation' to examine 'in a holistic and systematic way how anthropology shaped the relationship between state and society in India, and how it contributed to what we describe as India's "intellectual decolonization"' (https://www.theotherfromwithin.com/post/anthropology-state-and-society-relation-in-india accessed on 28 January 2021). In the short write-up published in the website of this British university project it was admitted that 'the history of anthropology in India is largely underdeveloped' and one of the reasons behind this underdevelopment lies in the focus on the role of the colonial ethnographers and the legacy of the colonial state. Interestingly, the authors of the project observed that Indian intellectuals found in anthropology a way to understand themselves and the problems of their society. They used their discipline to contest ideologies of racial superiority and to reconstruct what they saw as 'Indian tradition'. This process was not easy (ibid.).

We would of course wait for the results of research of the aforesaid mega-project funded by the Arts and Humanities Research Council of the British government.

Under this broader national and international intellectual context my aim is to search how the Indian anthropologists have undertaken serious researches on some of the major macro-level challenges (namely, *famine*, *resettlement of refugees* and *development-caused displacement*) encountered by the people of the newly independent nation by utilizing the methods and techniques of anthropology in the context of Indian reality. This is my point of departure, that I viewed as going beyond Talal Asad's celebrated book *Anthropology and the Colonial Encounter*, which analyzed and documented the ways anthropology was influenced by British colonialism (Asad 1973).

It should also be noted that Indian anthropology, unlike British, American and French anthropologies, grew under a colonial rule and it was a challenge for the Indian anthropologists to develop an anthropological tradition in a truly nationalist framework. Furthermore, Indian anthropology lacks studies on its own history and, more interestingly, the foreign/Western anthropologists who made remarkable contributions on the different aspects of Indian society and culture showed very little interest in writing a history of Indian anthropology. On the other hand, the Indian anthropologists, on their part, have only made sporadic attempts to write a comprehensive history of the discipline by taking into consideration the question of nation-building in post-independent India.

II

Research on the history of Anthropology in India, unlike Western countries, has not yet become a formidable tradition despite the fact that courses on the growth and development of Anthropology in India have been recommended at the undergraduate and postgraduate levels in the *Model Curriculum Development Report* of the University Grants Commission as early as 2001 (*Model Curriculum Development Report in Anthropology* 2001). There are, of course, a few published works on the history and the development of Anthropology in India, which include L.P. Vidyarthi's magnum opus entitled *Rise of Anthropology in India: A Social Science Orientation* (vols. I & II) published in 1978. In the first chapter of volume I of the book, Vidyarthi mentioned the 'sporadic attempts to review the researches in social anthropology in India' by scholars like S.C. Roy, D.N. Majumdar, G.S. Ghurye, S.C. Dube, N.K. Bose and S.C. Sinha (Vidyarthi 1978: 1-29). Vidyarthi, however, did not mention B.S. Guha's account of the history of Indian anthropology, which was published by the Indian Science Congress as early as 1938. In fact Guha's article entitled 'Progress of Anthropology in India during the Past Twenty-

Five Years' is the first comprehensive account on the history of Indian anthropology by an Indian anthropologist (Guha 1938: 300-35).[1] Quite significantly, Vidyarthi also could not find among these scholars any substantial attempt to search for a nationalist trend of social and cultural anthropology in India. Interestingly, both D.N. Majumdar and B.S. Guha in their articles on the progress of anthropology in India published in 1947 and 1949, respectively, emphasised the importance of anthropology as a holistic discipline in the task of building a new nation (Majumdar 1947: 1-31; Guha 1949: 607-13).

At this juncture, one should make it clear that Guha and Majumdar, unlike Vidyarthi, viewed anthropology as an integrated discipline comprising physical, social-cultural and prehistoric archaeology. Guha specialized as a physical anthropologist but did important research in social anthropology, and Majumdar, specialized as a social-cultural anthropologist, had also done work on physical anthropology and application of statistics in anthropology. Accordingly, in their articles on the history of anthropology in India, both Guha and Majumdar paid attention to physical and social-cultural anthropology for the growth and development of the discipline. The early interest of the scholars in anthropology to study the biological and cultural diversity of humankind in the Indian subcontinent was depicted not only by Guha and Majumdar in their historical accounts but also by other prominent anthropologists like Verrier Elwin and Nirmal Kumar Bose at a later period. One early example of biocultural synthesis in anthropology came from the original work done by Ramaprasad Chanda (1873-1942) who was the head of the department of anthropology at the University of Calcutta from 1920-1. R.P. Chanda was also a professional archaeologist and worked in the Archaeological Survey of India. He was one of the founders of the Indian Anthropological Institute and was its president during 1938-42. He represented India in the first international congress of anthropology held in London in 1934. Chanda had done original research on the somatic characters of Indian populations by using ancient Indian literature and challenged H.H. Risley's (the first census commissioner of India) theory on Indian races (*Journal of the Indian Anthropological Institute*, 1938 (1 & 2: i-iii). Another early example of doing research in biological and socio-cultural dimensions of humankind was Ramakrishna Mukherjee, a famous sociologist and social anthropologist belonging to the Marxist tradition. One should not forget that Ramkrishna Mukherjee did his doctoral work at Cambridge University in 1948 on the physical characteristics of the ancient populations of Sudan from the skeletal remains excavated from Jebel Moya (Mukherjee, Rao and Trevor 1955). Mukherjee's bio-cultural interest was also evident in his policy-oriented research on the problems of family planning in post-independent India (Mukherjee 1973). In an interesting memoriam published in 2016 in the *Economic and Political Weekly*, the famous sociologist and social anthropologist, T.N. Madan, recounted his first encounter with Ramkrishna Mukherjee in the early 1960s when the latter visited the department of anthropology of Lucknow University at the invitation of D.N. Majumdar as an 'expert member' of the committee of courses. Let me narrate the incident from the original text of Madan.

> I was a lecturer there, and after discussions among all faculty members, had been asked by Majumdar to prepare the outline of the social anthropology papers; other colleagues put together the physical anthropology and prehistory courses. Ramkrishna Mukherjee listened to the presentations with close concentration, and then reacted rather sharply, pointing out that what we had in hand were sets of topics; the concept of anthropology as a unified discipline was missing. 'Where are the connections?' he kept asking. What he advocated was a systematic (holistic) approach so as to bring out the 'logic' underlying the idea of anthropology as the empirical study of 'man' and 'culture' (Madan 2016: 28).

In 1946, Verrier Elwin was appointed as the deputy director of the Anthropological Survey of India under the directorship of B.S. Guha and he wrote an important article on the history of this governmental organization just a year after India's independence in 1948 in the international journal, *Man*. In the very beginning of this article, Elwin categorically mentioned:

> In India an enormous field of research, both theoretical and practical, lies before the anthropologist. The study of the physical characters of the people is still incomplete. . . . Not only do bodily measurements and characteristics require the fullest investigation, but these measurements should be accompanied by the study of deep-seated physiological characteristics, such as the percentage of blood groups in each race, which may well provide evidence of the original source from which particular tribes or races have sprung; of the effect of nutrition, and especially of an unbalanced nutrition, on the growth and proportions of the body and, possibly, also on its resistance to disease; and of the effect of climate on bodily structure and other physical characteristics—all still largely unexplored (Elwin 1948: 68).

In the same page Elwin stated:

> The fields of criminology, tribal art, primitive linguistics, the application of modern methods of psychological investigation to aboriginal people, the economics of the country-side not only offer a tempting subject of research to the scientist, but urgently require investigation if the inhabitants (and especially the more primitive inhabitants) of the country are to be administered with sympathy and understanding (ibid).

At this juncture, it may be pointed out that the narration of biosocial or biocultural research in anthropology in relation to nation-building is another neglected area in the writing of the history of anthropology in India. The historians of Indian anthropology invariably equated the discipline with only social anthropology despite the fact that the three major institutions of national importance were built up in which a substantial amount of anthropological research were carried out in an integrated biosocial framework under the leadership of eminent anthropologists. These three institutes were the department of anthropology at the University of Calcutta, Indian Statistical Institute and the Anthropological Survey of India.

A year before Elwin's article, Nabendu Datta-Majumdar, who succeeded Guha as director at the Anthropological Survey of India, wrote an article entitled 'Anthropology during the War' in another international journal, *American Anthropologist*, in which he meticulously reviewed the all-India scenario of the progress of anthropology and finally observed that, although research in the subject suffered most during the war, 'anthropology in India has progressed from an attempt to construct the history of culture to a realization of Indian needs and requirements. . .' (Datta-Majumder 1947: 164). Majumdar's conclusion was based on his brief but thorough reporting of anthropological researches from a holistic standpoint covering the three subfields of anthropology. I quote from Majumdar's essay:

> The years of the global war saw in India considerable progress in anthropometry and racial biology. . . This was the first time in India that a large-scale serological survey was carried along with anthropometric measurements. The data were analyzed by Prof. P.C. Mahalanobis FRS, of the Indian Statistical Institute, Calcutta . . . During the last five years the University School of Economics and Sociology, Bombay University, has continued its anthropological investigations by its students and teachers and, although anthropology is not taught there as an independent subject of study for the degree examination, a number of important investigations have been carried out by the students of the Sociology Department, some of which have not yet been printed due to the difficulty of securing paper and the restrictions on printing as wartime measures (Datta-Majumdar 1947: 160-1).

The last in the progress series was an exhaustive article entitled 'Progress of Anthropology and Archaeology' by N.K. Bose published by the Indian Science Congress Association in 1963. Bose, unlike Majumdar and Guha, did not deal with the role of anthropology in nation-building. After reviewing the then literature on the three subfields of anthropology, he instead dealt more with the possibilities of building an analytical and theoretical anthropology in the Indian context (Bose 1963: 1-48). Two brief surveys of 'Indian Anthropological Literature' which covered the period between 1946 and 1950 were published in the *Bulletin of the Department of Anthropology* (the then journal of the Anthropological Survey of India) in 1952 and 1953, respectively. These surveys contained detailed reports rather than critical reviews of the studies done by the Indian and foreign anthropologists in the country (*Bulletin of the Department of Anthropology* 1952: 154-9 and 1953: 112-19). Four years before the publication of Vidyarthi's book, a biographical sketch of the eminent Indian anthropologists was published by S.K. Ray, the then librarian of the Anthropological Survey of India, which also gave us some idea about the growth of anthropology in India (Ray 1974). Very recently, with the completion of 100 years of teaching anthropology in India, there is a resurgence of commemorating the works of the founders of Indian anthropology by the present-day anthropologists in India. Two books were already in preparation. One, authored by Sarthak Sengupta entitled *Architects of Anthropology in India* (2021) has already been published, and the other is by P.C. Joshi under the title *Fifty Indian Anthropologists* (Sengupta 2021; Joshi 2019), is forthcoming although neither of them is a book on the comprehensive history of the subject, let alone a search for the nationalist trends in Indian anthropology. Twelve years after the publication of the S.K. Roy book a calendrical account of the 'Landmarks of Indian Anthropology' was published in the official journal of the Anthropological Survey of India in 1986. In this calendar, a chronological account of the origin and development of Indian anthropology was given, which began with the year 1788 and ended in 1983. Quite interestingly, according to this calendar, out of the total number of 47 landmark events, 37 (more than 78 per cent) took place before the independence of India. Among these, 10 remaining landmark events during the post-independence period, only two events in 1951 were directly related to the process of nation-building, and those were the application of anthropological research findings in the (i) implementation of the community development project; and (ii) formulation of the panchayati raj system (Bose 1986: 74-6). The book, entitled *The History of the Anthropological Survey of India* (1991) edited by K.S. Singh, is a collection of valuable articles on studies done by the anthropologists in the various subfields but it also did not include any chapter on the history of Indian anthropology (Singh 1991). Singh, however, wrote an article, 'A Perspective on ASI', in 2000 in which he narrated the history of the establishment of the Anthropological Survey of India by the joint efforts of administrator-anthropologists—including J.P. Mills, J.H. Hutton, W.V. Grigson and W.G. Archer with anthropologists like Verrier Elwin and C. von Furer-Haimendorf, and, finally, by the single-minded pursuit of the idea by B.S. Guha (Singh 2000). Another article by Jayanta Sarkar written in 2003 highlighted the major research works in cultural anthropology undertaken by the Anthropological Survey of India since inception of the institution and this article also revealed the absence of an account of the history of the discipline (Sarkar 2003: 73-85). In a *Routledge Dictionary of Anthropologists* there is a very short description of the development of Indian anthropology based on already published Indian materials (Gaillard 2004).

All these aforementioned works contained a lot of useful data on the history of anthropology during the colonial and post-colonial periods but none of them ventured into a search for the growth of nationalist anthropological writings by the Indian anthropologists or the role of the anthropologists in nation-building in the pre- and post-independence periods. For example, in an important book *Anthropology on the March* (1963), containing 30 essays by Indian and foreign anthropologists and edited by Bala Ratnam, we do not find any article on the role of anthropologists in nation-building (Ratnam 1963). After more than a decade, two volumes on the latest position of research in various branches of anthropology in India, under the title *Anthropology in India* (1976), was published by the Anthropological Survey of India. The volumes (ed. Surajit Sinha and Hirendra Rakshit 1976) contained 21 articles on conventional and emerging areas of research in various branches of the subject but these volumes, too, did not include any chapter dealing with the history of anthropology in India, let alone on the problems of national integration and the role of anthropologists in nation-building. Much later, another book, *Anthropology in the East: Founders of Indian Sociology and Anthropology*, edited by Patricia Uberoi, Nandini Sundar and Satish Deshpande and published in 2007, contained separate biographical chapters on pioneering Indian anthropologists and sociologists by individual authors. Although not devoted to the search for the nationalist trends in Indian anthropology and sociology, this book contained interesting information on the activities and works of the pioneers of Indian anthropology and sociology in the pre- and post-independence periods. There were a number of perceptive articles which touched the different aspects of the history as well as the future of Indian anthropology but none of them attempted to write a comprehensive nationalist history of the discipline (See for example, Sinha 1967, 1971, 1974, 1978 & 1980; Singh 1987; Béteille 1997, 2000 & 2013; Sarana & Sinha 1976; Bhowmick 1984; Uberoi, Sundar and Deshpande 2000 & 2007; Srivastava 1999 & 2000; Bera 1995; Mehta 2002; Rao 2012; Sahay 1976; Joshi 2015; Das 2018). Roma Chatterji, in her brilliant article published in a book entitled *Asian Anthropology*, raised the question of Indianness in Indian anthropology and sociology but her point of departure was more on the reflexivity of Indian anthropologists with a tangential touch on the nationalist thinking among sociologists like M.N. Srinivas and T.N. Madan in the post-independence period (Chatterji 2005: 162-76). In the same book, another perceptive article by Vineeta Sinha dealt with the problem of 'indigenizing' anthropology in India and she observed that the accomplishments of the anthropologists in the nation-building tasks were miniscule (Sinha 2005: 139-61). Seven years later, another perceptive anthropologist, Vinay Kumar Srivastava, in his article 'Indian Anthropology Today,' noted that anthropologists are 'dispassionate observers' as well as 'citizens' and the 'state of contemporary anthropology' should be located in the dialectics between these two roles of the Indian anthropologists (Srivastava 2012: 359-73). Srivastava, too, did not explore the factual results of the dialectics between these two roles of the Indian anthropologists in the context of nation-building.

In a more recent article published in the *International Encyclopedia of Anthropology*, Satish Deshpande tried to distinguish between 'Anthropology of India' as viewed in the West and 'Anthropology in India' as practised by the Indian scholars. Deshpande observed perceptively:

> With the coming of Independence, everything seemed to change for the Indian academy. In keeping with the popular perceptions at the time, different academic fields and disciplines faced different futures in the new republic. . . Within the social sciences, economics was by far the most favoured discipline since it was seen as leading the fight against poverty. History, too, was viewed with favour since it could now devote itself to writing a retrospective biography of the nation. As the discipline that would presumably monitor and document the political life of the world's newest and largest democracy, political science, too, seemed to have a secure future. In sharp contrast, Indian sociology and, especially, anthropology seemed at odds with nationalism and the requirements of a national state. More than any other discipline, it was anthropology that had to reinvent itself in Independent India (Deshpande 2018: 5).

Deshpande, however, has not made any attempt to explore the pioneering efforts of anthropologists in the task of nation-building through a search in the literature. His list of the areas of concern within anthropology in India has not taken into account the remarkable contributions of the Indian anthropologists on famine, partition, resettlement of refugees and development caused displacement by big dams and industries in the post-independence period of India.

It is interesting to recall here a paper presented by P. Padmanabha, then Registrar General of the Indian Census Organization in the Xth International Congress of Anthropological and Ethnological Sciences held in Delhi in 1978. While narrating the shift in the orientation of census data in the post-independence period he noted:

> After the independence of India in 1947, the orientation of census data under went considerable change to meet the new requirements of social planning and development. The shifts from the needs of administration of a colonial government to that of a national government for economic

> re-construction and welfare measures brought in its wake changes in data requirement. . . . The end of British rule was accompanied by partition of India, resulting in large-scale international migrations and displacement of people in the sub-continent whose rehabilitation itself was a colossal task. In the light of these developments and economic upheavals the data relevant to policies for the re-construction of economy naturally received the first priority during the 1951 census which was the first census after independence (Padmanabha 1978: 8-9).

The Registrar General, however, remained silient on the displacement caused by big dams and industries in the post-independence period of the country, which were studied by the anthropologists.

Under this wider intellectual scenario one may recall Surajit Sinha's perceptive review of Nirmal Kumar Bose's ideas about the development of an Indian tradition of anthropology through the studies on urgent problems of post-independent India, and Sinha emphasized the dangers of using borrowed ideas from the West (Sinha 1967: 1707-9). Despite his repeated insistence for Indian anthropology, Surajit Sinha too, however, did not delve much deeper into a historical search for nationalist trends in Indian anthropology. He seemed to have restricted himself around the thoughts of Nirmal Kumar Bose only while looking at the nationalist tradition in Indian anthropology. N.K. Bose's research endeavours, on the other hand, were largely influenced by the American cultural diffusionists, like Franz Boas, A.L. Kroeber and Clark Wissler (Bose 1953).

III

Under these facts and circumstances, the conceptual framework of my discourse is derived from a critical and selective reading of the anthropological texts produced by Indian anthropologists. This reading of the history of Indian anthropology is based on two sources. One source is the reading of the original texts by pioneering anthropologists which were committed to various tasks of nation-building and the other is the reading of literature by anthropologists who regarded early Indian anthropology as simply following the Western tradition. These two readings of the texts are juxtaposed to write a new and critical history of Indian anthropology, which I have designated as the 'new discourse' in the title of an earlier occasional paper (see Guha 2018a: 3-41).

The overall planning of this book is designed on the basis of the previous works done by the author on the history of anthropological research in India. It was also based on the hypothesis that a nationalist tradition of anthropological research could be discernible in India. Accordingly, the methodology of the research is exploratory and involved intensive reading of the literature which carried this nationalist tradition. Reading of analytical papers and critical essays rather than ethnographic monographs on single communities by the pioneers was taken up to construct this new discourse.

IV

In this book, I have argued that, while criticizing Indian anthropology the critics mostly ignored the studies done by the pioneers of the disciplines, which were relevant at the national level and directed towards the welfare and betterment of the underprivileged sections of our country. I will make a list of some of the remarkable scholars of the early Indian anthropology who, though they worked during the colonial period, tried to build up a nationalist tradition of anthropology. All of the following anthropologists were born in India in the nineteenth and early twentieth centuries, and applied their knowledge in anthropology and sociology for the cause of the marginalized and exploited tribals and other underprivileged and deprived sections of the Indian population. Although, these anthropologists benefited from the theory and methodology of the Western scholars, they tried to generate an Indian discourse by using this knowledge to develop the subject in order to meet the bigger challenges encountered by the country at the time of independence and in the early decades after the event. But before I move into the domain of nationalist anthropology, I narrate another interesting story in the development of anthropology in India, which is 'Hindu anthropology'.

V

On the reverse side of the critiques, there also existed a view that an Indian form of anthropology could be discerned in many ancient Indian texts and scriptures before the advent of a colonial anthropology introduced by the European scholars, administrators and missionaries in the Indian subcontinent. As early as 1938, Jogendra Chandra Ghosh (a reputed scholar in ancient Indian history who contributed in the prestigious journal of the Bhandarkar Oriental Research Institute in the 1930s) , in his interesting article 'Hindu Anthropology' published in the *Anthropological Papers* (*New Series*), no. 5 of the University of Calcutta, tried to show that, before the sixth century BC, the Hindus innovated various measurements on human body and its parts which, in European terms, was anthropometry, an important branch of physical anthropology. Ghosh began his article with the following words.

> Anthropology is one of the modern progressive sciences. Anthropometry and ethnology are the two important branches of this science. We shall here give some facts to show that the Hindus had their anthropometry and ethnology from a very early period (Ghosh 1938: 27).

Ghosh further pointed out that the earliest record of those anthropometric measurements was found in *Susruta Samhita*, a medical treatise written by the ancient Hindus. He also held that the ancient Hindus had their own notion of ethnology, and its first expression was found in *Rigveda* in which 'races' were classified on the basis of their skin colour. Suffice it is to say that Ghosh was implying that this 'racial theory' was to become a major theme in later-day Western anthropology.

Another later proponent of 'Hindu anthropology' was the famous anthropologist, Nirmal Kumar Bose (1901-72), who was a one-time secretary to Mahatma Gandhi and himself a committed nationalist. Bose, in his earliest textbook entitled *Cultural Anthropology* published in 1929, made a novel attempt to show that the ancient Hindus in their scriptures classified the desires or needs of human beings into *artha* (economic), *kama* (sexual) and *moksha* (spiritual), almost in the fashion of later-day functional anthropologists of the West. Bose probably held that the Hindus, like the Western anthropologists, had their own scheme of understanding human nature and behaviour which existed since long. Bose later proposed a theory in Indian anthropology entitled the 'Hindu Method of Tribal Absorption' which helped to induce the tenets of 'Hindu anthropology' more effectively among the successive generation of anthropologists in India. The idea was first proposed in a paper in the Indian Science Congress in 1941. Bose's proposal was based on his short field trips among the Juang tribal community of the Pal Lahara region of then Orissa.

The essence of the theory was that the tribals who had come into contact with their powerful caste Hindu neighbours gradually lost their own tribal identity and were given a low-caste status within the Hindu fold. This idea became very popular and acceptable among the mainstream Indian anthropologists and Bose's paper turned into a compulsory text in the curriculum of Indian anthropology. There was hardly any question or re-study in the Juang area to recheck Bose's proposition and the idea took deep roots in the minds of Indian anthropologists for generations. The university and college students of India who studied anthropology were taught the theory of 'Hindu Method of Tribal Absorption' as an established sociological fact. Bose's nationalist ideas, therefore, were based on his anthropological views of vertical integration of society in which the Brahminical ideals were at the topmost position. Sociologist Pradip Bose neatly summarized the essence of Nirmal Kumar Bose's Hindu nationalism in a brilliant manner.

> ... Bose' depiction of Hinduism describes a process which vertically integrates various groups into a social structure administered and guided

by Brahminical ideals and values. The same vision of the absorptive power of Hinduism explains his argument that tribals were successfully assimilated into the Hindu fold. In a way, Bose, like the early Orientalist writers, projected Indian social history as essentially the history of Hinduism, or of the assimilation of non-Hindu groups into Hindu society (Bose 2007: 326).

Therefore, under Bose's scheme, Hinduization of the tribals was accepted as an obvious and inevitable process which also helped to overlook any possibility of protest by the tribals against Brahminical imposition in any form. It also helped to hide the exploitation and subjugation of the tribals by the Hindus. Later, another theory proposed by M.N. Srinivas, one of the doyens of Indian sociology and social anthropology, reinforced the superiority of the Brahmins by showing that the lower-castes always tried to imitate and emulate the life-style of the twice-born castes. This theory came to be known as 'Sanskritization' and also became an essential part of the college and university curriculum in Indian anthropology and sociology. A lone Indian sociologist Surendra Munshi, criticized both N.K. Bose and M.N. Srinivas in his brilliant article, 'Tribal absorption and Sanskritization in Hindu society', published in the prestigious journal, *Contributions to Indian Sociology* in unequivocal terms.

> My more serious criticism against Bose and Srinivas is that, lacking a general sociological theory of society and social change within the framework of which empirical data are to be collected, interpreted and transcended, they end up with the transformation of the object of study into a theory that has conditioned the study itself. In other words, in their concern with the ideal sphere, they are compelled to accept the ruling ideas of the society, past and present, for providing them with the interpretation of the corresponding empirical reality studied by them. In sum, their analysis is ideological (Munshi 1979: 304).

Munshi, however, did not deal with the inconsistencies and lack of fit between the data collected by N.K. Bose and the theoretical generalizations made by him in his 'Hindu Method of Tribal Absorption' paper. Since the publication of the twin ideas, Indian anthropology and sociology revolved round the 'Hindu Method of Tribal Absorption' and 'Sanskritization', and under the strong influence of Bose and Srinivas, anthropology and sociology in India came to be oriented towards the study of Hindu religious and higher-caste superiority.[2] For example, Tarak Chandra Das' view on Indian anthropology and the tribal society was completely different from that of Bose and Srinivas, although the former's work did not receive due attention by the anthropologists in India.[3] Ironically, despite being an excellent field worker and ethnographer, Das' ideas did not receive much attention even from his famous students, like Surajit Sinha, B.K. Roy Burman, and André Béteille.[4] The path set by the doyens left little scope for a secular and materialist Indian anthropology (Guha 2018: 105-110). The search for the counter movements against Hinduisation and ethnographies of anti-acculturative processes in Indian anthropology and sociology was marginalized to a large extent. The Western scholars who came to India in the post-independence period, too, mainly studied caste and village level dynamics as well as Indian civilization under the framework of a high-caste Hindu order which again added force to the models generated by Bose and Srinivas. The growth of a secular and national anthropology in India was nipped in the bud. Indian anthropology became Hinduized, religious and, at the same time, Westernized. Indian anthropologists forgot that the development of a national anthropology also required a secular and indigenous approach to the problems of nation-building. The tenets of 'Hindu anthropology' are still haunting some of the Indian anthropologists. Thus, Ajit Kumar Danda, former director of the Anthropological Survey of India and the chairman of the Indian National Confederation and Academy of Anthropologists (INCAA), claimed in one of the professional journals of the subject, *Journal of the Indian Anthropological Society*, in 2017:

One of the earliest *Smritis Manava Dharmasharstra* (literally, *The Sacred Science of Man*), dates approximately 1350 BC . . . is perhaps the most ancient text in anthropology ever produced anywhere on the earth. It is claimed to be more than 1,000 years older than the first application of the word anthropology, as such, which is believed to have been used for the first time by Aristotle (384-22 BC) (Danda 2017: 6).

Nowhere in his article entitled 'Anthropology in Contemporary India' could Danda discern a secular and nationalist stream of thought in the history of Indian anthropology. He had only seen anthropology as an 'academic discipline' (the Westernized tradition) and a 'body of knowledge' (the ancient Hindu tradition), and thus failed to appreciate the secular, materialist and nationalist tradition of anthropological thought in India. Suffice it to say that in his 'body of knowledge' type of anthropology, there was hardly any place for the adivasis, the dalits and the *lokayata* traditions of thought. To give an example. The monumental work, entitled *Lokayata: A Study of Ancient Indian Materialism* (1959), New Delhi: People's Publishing House, written by the famous Marxist philosopher Debiprasad Chattopadhyaya did not find a mention in Danda's long text on Indian philosophy. Danda, however, unlike his predecessor Jogendra Chandra Ghosh, did not use the term 'Hindu anthropology' but his intention was clear, which was to push an upper-caste and Sanskritic tradition of thought in the academia under the cover of anthropology as a 'body of knowledge' (Guha 2019a: 54-168).

I would conclude this chapter with the following statement. The dominant discourse in Indian anthropology was saturated with a higher-caste Hindu ideology by the idea of the Hindu method of tribal absorption proposed by Bose in the 1940s in such a way that nobody questioned the nature of the data collected by Bose himself which, by any standard, stood on methodologically unsound foundations. The then ethnographic discourse generated by Das that recorded the counter-processes of de-hinduization and maintenance of ethnic identity by the economically and socially subjugated and marginalised tribals was largely pushed into oblivion and overlooked by anthropologists in India.

NOTES

1. In fact, B.S. Guha, in his 1938 Science Congress article, provided detailed information on the works done by the anthropologists on India which included not only social-cultural anthropology but also in physical anthropology and prehistory.
2. It is interesting to note in this connection that, in a more recent period, the idea of an Islamic anthropology has also been proposed by some anthropologists. In an article entitled 'Defining Islamic Anthropology' published in the prestigious *Royal Anthropological Institute Newsletter* (*RAIN*), Akbar S. Ahmed noted that the 'issue of Islamic anthropology has been raised by Muslim anthropologists' and it also posed 'serious questions of a philosophical as well as an anthropological nature' (Ahmed 1984: 2-4).
3. Interestingly, T.C. Das's obituary was not published in any journal of anthropology in India. Only *Sociological Bulletin* published the obituary of this great nationalist anthropologist (*Sociological Bulletin* 1964).
4. In a more recent period, Béteille, however, corrected himself about his lesser-known teacher, Tarak Chandra Das. In his autobiographical memoir entitled *Ourselves and Others* published in the *Annual Review of Anthropology*, he recalled his experiences of studying anthropology at the University of Calcutta in the following manner. I quote Béteille (2013): 'Things in the department of Anthropology were organised on a small scale, and they moved at a slow pace. The teachers were easily accessible to their students. One of those who taught us about society and culture, T.C. Das, was meticulous and conscientious, and had a vast store of detailed ethnographic knowledge.'

CHAPTER 2

Conceptual Framework of the Study and Methodology

I

The conceptual framework of this study is derived from a critical reading of the history of Indian anthropology. This reading of the history of Indian anthropology is based on two sources. One source is the reading of the original texts by pioneering anthropologists who were committed to various tasks of nation-building and the other is the reading of the literature by anthropologists who regarded early Indian anthropology as simply following the Western tradition. These two readings of the texts are juxtaposed to write a critical history of Indian anthropology.

Under this conceptual framework the aims and objectives of the study are enumerated below:

(i) To investigate the nationalist trends in the writings of Indian anthropologists both in the pre- and post-independence periods, which were aimed at serving the Indian nation.

(ii) To collect biographical and other information on the anthropologists who attempted to develop a nationalist tradition in Indian anthropology, rather than blindly following the Western anthropologists.

(iii) To collect historical data on the social commitment and humanistic roles of the anthropologists of India who viewed anthropology as a tool for national development.

(iv) To write a history of nationalist anthropology in India.

(v) To use this nationalist history of Indian anthropology for building our nation in the present context.

(vi) To enrich the present syllabi and curriculum of anthro pology in India by using the knowledge gained on the nationalist tradition of Indian anthropology through this research.

II

RESEARCH QUESTIONS AND HYPOTHESIS

My hypothesis in this research is that a nationalist trend in anthropology along with the colonial tradition was also growing during the pre- and post-independence periods in India and this trend was characterized by the works of the anthropologists who were socially committed and contributed to nation-building through their analytical writings and research. Under this broad hypothesis, the research questions are as follows.

(i) Who were the nationalist anthropologists in pre-independence India?
(ii) What were the areas of concern of the nationalist anthropologists in pre-independence India?
(iii) What were the visions of the nationalist anthropologists in pre-independence India?
(iv) How were the nationalist anthropologists were trying to develop anthropology and anthropological institutes in post-independence India?
(v) Was there any attempt by the nationalist anthropologists to develop anthropological theories suited to the Indian reality?

III

SCOPE AND METHODOLOGY

Scope

Analytical essays or parts of ethnographic monographs, rather than descriptive and/or simple ethnographic treatises, devoted to the role of anthropology in nation-building have come under the purview of this research. So, Sarat Chandra Roy's pioneering article, 'An Indian Outlook on Anthropology' (Roy 1938) and Tarak Chandra Das' sectional presidential address at the Indian Science Congress, entitled 'Cultural Anthropology in the Service of the Individual and the Nation', delivered in 1941, apart from his novel paper on museum building in independent India, would be more important as data sources for the purpose of this research rather than Roy and Das' classical ethnographic monographs on the Mundas and Purum Kukis of Manipur (Das 1941). In the same vein, the Indian Science Congress' sectional presidential lecture entitled 'The place of human biology in anthropology and its utility in the service of the nation' by Sasanka Sekhar Sarkar was more important than Sarkar's classical works on racial classification in India. Another example is Verrier Elwin's comprehensive essay on the 'History of Anthropological Survey of India' published in 1948 (Elwin 1948). His classical monographs on the Muria Gonds of Bastar did not come under the scope of this research.

The second group of anthropological works which have come within the ambit of my investigation were the ones conducted on a burning problem of the country which has had tremendous bearing on nation-building. For example, the rare and unique research of Tarak Chandra Das on the Bengal famine (1949) and on social tensions among the refugees (1959) by Biraja Sankar Guha fall under this category (Guha 2017, 2016a, 2010, 2011). Quite offbeat and almost forgotten but original, an article written by B.R. Ambedkar on the origin of the caste system in India, presented in an anthropology seminar at Columbia University in 1916, will also be relooked in this context of nationalistic trends in anthropology, since it sharply differed with the explanations provided by Western as well as Marxist and non-Marxist Indian scholars (like N.K. Bose and M.N. Srinivas) on the caste system in India (Ambedkar 1917). I have already written an article and presented a paper in a national seminar organized by the Anthropological Survey of India on this theme (Guha 2017a & 2016c).

The third group of anthropological works which were investigated under this objective comprised those that were done to serve the nation with a direct policy motive. For example, the policy research with solid recommendations on the adverse impacts of displacement caused by dams and industrialization in Odisha and Maharashtra during the 1960s by anthropologists like B.K. Roy Burman (1968), and Irawati Karve and Jai Nimbkar (1969). These works were not only pioneering in nature but were also characterized by a kind of social commitment and humanism which made them notable in the history of nationalist thinking in Indian anthropology.

I have already published a book and some articles, and also presented papers in seminars through which the theme of nationalist trends in anthropology has been pursued in various forums (Guha 2017b, 2016a & b).

RESEARCH DESIGN AND METHODOLOGY

The overall planning of this research is designed on the basis of the previous works done by the scholars on the history of anthropological research in India. It is also based on the hypothesis that a nationalist tradition of anthropological research is discernible in India. Accordingly, the methodology of the research was exploratory and involved intensive reading of the literature which carried this nationalist tradition. Readings of analytical papers and critical essays, rather than plain ethnographies by the pioneers, were more important in this endeavour. Ethnographies were read in a critical manner to understand and explore underlying policy implications towards nation-building and the social commitment of individual authors.

COLLECTION OF DATA

Anthropological literature in the Central Library of the Anthropological Survey of India is the major source for the collection of data for this book. Search through the Internet and JSTOR was also undertaken to collect and read the relevant literature.

IV

RELEVANCE, ANTICIPATED OUTCOMES AND PROPOSED OUTPUTS FROM THE RESEARCH

RELEVANCE OF THE STUDY

This study has immense significance, not only for the reconstruction of the development of anthropology in India, but also for learning lessons and drawing inspiration from the socially committed and nationalist traditions of anthropology by the present generation. Another significance of the study that is no less important, would be its contribution towards the enrichment of the current curriculum of anthropology throughout the country.

ANTICIPATED OUTCOMES

The present-day problems, and the needs of the society and the country, require the attention of these anthropologists who viewed the problems from a holistic perspective. The insights of the anthropologists who were pioneers in this country are relevant till today since they viewed the problems of social tension, culture change, displacement and other burning issues which still plague the country. Above all, what is needed today is a more humane and sympathetic approach towards the minorities, underprivileged, exploited and the marginalized, and the discovery of the nationalist trends in Indian anthropology would strengthen this humane and practical approach to policy making in the present period.

PROPOSED OUTPUT

This library-cum-archival research to explore the nationalist trends in Indian anthropology during the pre- and post-independence periods would enrich our knowledge on a hitherto-untouched area in the history of Indian anthropology. The benefits of the knowledge gained through this research would be two-fold. On the one hand, results of this research could be incorporated in the post-graduate curriculum under the rubric: 'nationalist tradition in Indian anthropology'. On the other hand, the findings of the research would help to inspire the present generation of anthropologists to undertake studies on the current socially relevant problems of the country in the context of making life in India more meaningful as was being attempted by our founding generation of anthropologists. Last but not the least, the results of this study would also generate further research to probe more deeply and critically the history of Indian anthropology, a task which has not yet been developed as a tradition in the pedagogy of this discipline.

CHAPTER 3

Did the Early Indian Anthropologists Follow their Colonial Masters?

I

The colonial connection of anthropology, particularly British social anthropology, virtually began with the publication of the famous book, *Anthropology & the Colonial Encounter*, edited by Talal Asad, in 1973. Asad noted that 'social anthropology emerged as a distinctive discipline at the beginning of the colonial era', although most of the professional anthropologists showed a 'strange reluctance' to study the colonial connection of social anthropology (Asad 1973: 14-15). More than a decade later, an Indian social anthropologist and sociologist, Jaganath Pathy, in his article published in the *Economic and Political Weekly*, critiqued anthropology, in general, and third world development anthropology, in particular, for serving the colonial and imperial powers (Pathy 1981: 623-7). Both Asad and Pathy, however, had their counterpoints, too! Asad, for example, stated at the end of his introduction:

> I believe it is a mistake to view social anthropology in the colonial era as primarily an aid to colonial administration, or as the simple reflection of colonial ideology. I say this not because I subscribe to the anthropological establishment's comfortable view of itself, but because bourgeois consciousness, of which social anthropology is merely one fragment, has always contained within itself profound contradictions and ambiguities and, therefore, the potentialities for transcending itself (Asad 1973: 18).

Pathy, after quoting Mao-Zedong on the 'underlying principle of knowledge', concluded:

In the pursuit, the anthropologists should shed their value neutrality and stop opposing large scale changes. The need is to transform anthropology from being an instrument of domination of the oppressors to becoming an instrument of liberation of the oppressed (Pathy 1981: 627).

Neither Asad nor Pathy made any attempt to show how social anthropology or anthropology in countries in the post-colonial era could be put to use in a truly nationalist spirit to serve the interests of the oppressed by transcending the colonial hangover.

In this context, it would be interesting to note that in India the critical assessment of the colonial legacy of anthropology by the anthropologists had an older beginning than that advanced by Talal Asad and Jaganath Pathy. Let me begin my narrative on the critique.

There is a standard critique of Indian anthropology advanced by some Indian anthropologists. The critics opined that Indian anthropology was the product of a colonial tradition and the Indian anthropologists, for various reasons, followed their colonial and neocolonial masters in one way or the other. Let me try to arrange the critiques of Indian anthropology in a chronological manner.

II

A CHRONOLOGICAL DESCRIPTION OF CRITIQUES

1. As early as 1952, Nirmal Kumar Bose, in a significant article entitled, 'Current research projects in Indian anthropology', published in *Man in India* enumerated the research projects undertaken by the department of Anthropology, Government of India (the former name of the Anthropological Survey of India) and the anthropology departments at Calcutta, Madras, Lucknow, Delhi, Gauhati and Osmania Universities. Bose's investigation was exhaustive and based on written replies from the heads of the aforementioned institutions. After reviewing the overall scenario, he concluded:

There does not seem to be any problem which Indian anthropologists have made peculiarly their own. Anthropologists in our country have, on the whole, followed the tracks beaten by anthropologists in the more powerful countries of the West. What they do, we generally try to repeat on the Indian soil (Bose 1952: 133).

Bose, however, ended with the positive note that there were exceptions to the above generalization and, if Indian anthropologists could work independently on Indian problems, there was still sign of hope. Just 10 years later, N.K. Bose published another article, 'Researches in Indian anthropology', in the same journal in which he turned the attention of the readers from applied to 'certain fundamental problems in anthropology' and mentioned about the researches done by social anthropologists on the persistence of the caste system. Along with this, Bose mentioned the anthropometric surveys carried out by physical anthropologists at the all-India level as another type of fundamental research and he found young anthropologists at the Anthropological Survey of India to be 'first-class workers' (Bose 1962a: 179).

2. After Bose, his famous student Surajit Sinha, in his insightful article published in the *Journal of the Indian Anthropological Society* (hereafter *JIAS*) in 1971, observed that, despite considerable growth in research publications and professional human power in social and cultural anthropology during the last 100 years, Indian anthropologists largely remained dependent on Western and colonial traditions (Sinha 1971: 1-14). In continuation of his pertinent examination of the colonial dependence of Indian anthropology, Sinha contributed a full chapter entitled 'India: A Western Apprentice' in a book, *Anthropology: Ancestors and Heirs*, edited by the Marxist anthropologist Stanley Diamond in 1980 and published by Mouton. In that article, Sinha discussed 'the process of naturalization of the different strands of Western anthropological traditions' and finally ended with the following pessimistic note:

For some time, the proliferation of trained manpower, random efforts at catching up with the latest developments in the West and a general increase in the number of publications will characterize the development of Indian anthropology (Sinha 1980: 281).

Trained by both Nirmal Kumar Bose and Tarak Chandra Das and also at a later stage by Robert Redfield, Sinha was exposed to a wide arena of global and national anthropology. He completed his major works on the relationship between tribe and caste in the context of Indian civilization as well as state formation by mid-1960s. A closer view of his published works revealed that he first presented the critical idea on Indian anthropology in a Wenner-Gren Foundation conference held in New York in 1968 (Sinha 1968). In fact, Sinha's self-critical views on the growth of Indian social science, in general, and anthropology and sociology, in particular, could be traced back to his article entitled, 'Involvement in social change: a plea for own ideas', published in the radical social science journal, *Economic and Political Weekly*, as early as 1967 (Sinha 1967: 1707-9). In this article, Sinha stated quite categorically:

> A scholarly tradition of leaning heavily, if not abjectly, on ideas borrowed from the West is growing in this country. This is clear from the post-independence writings of a large number of Indian social scientists and the research policies of some of our modem research institutions. The borrowed ideas and concepts, when accepted uncritically, obscure the major issues involved in planned social change and stand in the way of posing the right kind of questions in the study of social change (ibid 1707).

Sinha pursued this critique of Indian social science by converging his attack on Indian anthropology in the subsequent articles. Taking note of his earlier article in *JIAS*, Sinha, in his 'foreword to the precious book, *Bibliographies of Eminent Indian Anthropologists* (1974), written by Shyamal Kumar Ray, made this remark.

> '. . . there was a general reluctance among Indian scholars to take due note of the research publications of Indian pioneers and contemporaries. As a result, research endeavours of Indian scholars tend to be derivative,

leaving the responsibilities of breaking new grounds exclusively to Western scholars (Sinha 1974: iii).'

Although Sinha praised N.K. Bose and T.C. Das at the individual levels for their insight and ethnography, respectively, the critiques advanced by Sinha in his 1967, 1971 and 1980 articles on the overall achievement of Indian anthropology was quite pessimistic and distressing. For him, there was hardly any sign of an independent, let alone nationalist, Indian anthropology. In his article entitled, 'Urgent Problems for Research in Social and Cultural Anthropology in India: Perspectives and Suggestions', published in *Sociological Bulletin* in 1968, Sinha identified three distinct social anthropological 'vantage points' to approach the urgent problems in India, which were: (i) study of 'primitive groups' of tribes, (ii) study of human groups for the theoretical understanding of Indian society, and (iii) anthropological study of problems urgently needed for national reconstruction and development. Curiously, Sinha left the third area untouched for the purpose of the paper (Sinha 1968: 123-31). It was not clear why he had done so and what purpose prevented him to undertake discussion on this vital area. More interestingly, a few years later, Sinha wrote in the foreword of the book, *Bibliographies of Eminent Indian Anthropologists:*

> We are also impressed by the fact that these pioneering scholars, often working under severe limitations of resources, were engaged in lifelong endeavour in their particular areas of academic interest. Each of them demonstrated a rare quality of mental independence while living most of their lives under colonial rule (Sinha 1974: iii).

Surajit Sinha never came up with a comprehensive and overall review of the results of the 'mental independence' of his predecessors who lived their 'lives under colonial rule'. He seemed to satisfy himself only with the praise of N.K. Bose and occasionally T.C. Das.

3. Next to Sinha came the critique of Amitabha Basu and Suhas Biswas who held faculty positions at the prestigious Indian Statistical Institute at Kolkata. In their article, '*Is Indian Anthro-*

pology Dead/Dying?' published in the *Journal of the Indian Anthropological Society*, they raised the question of social relevance of Indian anthropology squarely and concluded that the subject was either dead or dying in the post-colonial period (Basu and Biswas 1980: 1-4). More interestingly, some commentators (e.g. V. Balakrishnan, P.P. Majumder and D. Piplai, 1980, pp. 4-5, 9-10 & 11-12) in the paper disagreed with Basu and Biswas and argued that anthropology in India was very much useful for the ruling and privileged classes and might not be useful for the masses!

4. One of the most sarcastic critiques of Indian social anthropology was written by A.C. Sinha in his article, 'Indian Social Anthropology and Its Cambridge Connections', published in 1991 in *The Eastern Anthropologist*. In this article, Sinha argued, and with archival evidence, that many of the Indian doyens of social anthropology and sociology depended largely on British anthropologists for advancement in their personal careers. In Sinha's list, there were names of B.S. Guha, M.N. Srinivas, Ramkrishna Mukherjee, D.N. Majumdar, S.C. Dube, and N. Prasad. I quote him below:

> One finds pompous Guha, the recently-appointed academic bureaucrat, looking for approval to his uncertain blueprints. One also notes that Srinivas, Mukherjee, Majumdar, Dube, Narmadeshwar Prasad—all aspiring sociologists and social anthropologists—they would be mandarins—who were destined to steer the Indian sociological establishment for at least three decades in post-1950 period—behaving in the same 'comical and pathetic ways' for securing an approving nod from their Cambridge establishment (Sinha 1991: 351-2).

Sinha, however, did not explore further to see how this dependence on the Cambridge establishment influenced the academic contributions of the Indian social anthropologists.

5. Celebrated social anthropologist and sociologist André Béteille, in one of his articles published in *Sociological Bulletin* in 1997, wrote:

> In India, each generation of sociologists seems eager to start its work on a clean slate, with little or no attention to the work done before. This

amnesia about the work of their predecessors is no less distinctive of Indian sociologists than their failure to innovate (Béteille 1997: 98).

Béteille's observation on Indian sociologists, however, was not novel. Long before his pronouncement, N.K. Bose and Surajit Sinha critiqued Indian anthropologists almost in a similar manner, which I have already mentioned.

6. After about two decades of Sinha, another anthropologist, Biswanath Debnath, in his article published in the *Economic and Political Weekly*, castigated Indian anthropologists for failing to evolve their own tradition and blindly following the footsteps of the colonial masters by studying small, isolated and marginal tribal communities and their process of integration in the mainstream Indian civilizations (Debnath 1999: 3110-14). Almost the same kind of sharp criticism of the alleged neo-colonial bias in Indian anthropology can be found in the writings of J.J. Roy-Burman in 2011 (Roy-Burman 2011).

7. In a recent article published in *Economic and Political Weekly*, Vivek Kumar, a professor of sociology at Jawaharlal Nehru University, in his article, 'How Egalitarian Is Indian Sociology?', observed a caste bias in Indian sociology and social anthropology (Kumar 2017: 33-9).

Interestingly, none of these critiques were forwarded by any Western anthropologist or sociologist and all the critiques were put forward by professionals who earned or are earning their livelihood by practising sociology and/or anthropology in India.

8. In a more academic vein, R. Srivatsan argued in his *Economic and Political Weekly* article that the dominant discourse among anthropologists and sociologists on tribal policy in India had changed little from the colonial times to the emergence of nationalism in the early post-independent years (Srivatsan 1986: 1986-99).

The critics of Indian anthropology (Bose, Sinha, Basu, Béteille and Debnath) and the proponents of 'Hindu anthropology' (Ghosh, Bose and Danda) ignored the materialistic, socially committed, secular and nationalist trends of Indian anthropology which were growing in the hands of some remarkable anthropologists before and after the independence of the country (Guha 2018a: 105-10 and 154-68 & 2019a). The critics have only followed the convenient way of taking down the pioneers instead of studying the socially committed works of the latter and this was one of the reasons that Indian anthropologists failed to honour their nationalist predecessors and depended more on the wisdom of the Western scholars. At best, the critics have only paid lip service to those nationalist pioneers of the discipline.

CHAPTER 4

Nationalist Anthropology in India: Origin and Growth

I

In an important book entitled *Anthropology in the East*, Patricia Uberoi, Nandini Sundar and Satish Deshpande, in the sub-section 'Nationalism and the Nation-State' of the introduction commented:

> We are yet to form a detailed picture of the ways in which nationalism exerted its influence in shaping Indian sociology and social anthropology. To be sure, almost every historical account of the discipline, whether it concerns an individual, an institution or the discipline at large, makes mention of this factor . . . (Uberoi, Sundar & Deshpande 2007: 38).

In the discussion that followed the above-quoted opening statement, the authors admitted two important points, viz., that the question of nationalism occupied a 'very wide spectrum' and that no Indian anthropologist or sociologist could oppose nationalism. I do not claim that I have been able to cover the whole range of the nationalist spectrum of Indian anthropology, but I could discover only some of the notable nationalist anthropologists and highlight their works in some detail just as a beginning.

Along with the colonial tradition, a nationalist trend in Indian anthropology could also be discerned which was growing during the pre-and post-independence periods in India and this trend was characterized by the works of the anthropologists who were socially committed and contributed to nation-building through their analytical writings and research (Guha 2018a: 8).

These anthropologists learned the methodology of the discipline from the West but did not become blind followers of Europe and America and they also did not want to derive their anthropology from the religious scriptures of the ancient Hindus. Instead, they visualized an Indian character of anthropology, which according to them, could be used in nation-building, a task which finally could not be developed into full maturity by their own successors. Let me explain with the aid of examples.

In 1938, the same year in which Jogendrachandra Ghosh wrote the article, 'Hindu Anthropology' in a Calcutta University journal, one of the founding fathers of Indian anthropology, Sarat Chandra Roy, wrote an article entitled, 'An Indian Outlook on Anthropology' in *Man*, the journal of the Royal Anthropological Institute of Great Britain and Ireland. This article can be regarded as one of the pioneering ones in the nationalist tradition of Indian anthropology. In this article, Roy not only critically evaluated the major theories developed in Western anthropology, like evolutionism, diffusionism and functionalism, in a refreshing authentic first initiative, but also made a novel attempt to synthesize the ideas of ancient Indian philosophers with Western anthropological concepts. According to Roy, the essence of Indian thought lay in the subjective process of 'sympathetic immersion' in other cultures and societies and this could be combined with the objective approach of Western anthropology. I quote Roy:

> Thus the objective methods of investigation of cultural data have to be helped out, not only by historical imagination and a background of historical and geographical facts, but also by a subjective process of self-forgetting absorption or meditation (*dhyana*) and *intuition* born of sympathetic immersion in, and self-identification with, the society under investigation.

The spread of this attitude by means of anthropological study can surely be a factor helping forward the large *unity-in-diversity-through-sympathy* that seems to an Indian mind to be the inner meaning of the process of human evolution, and the hope of a world perplexed by a multitude of *new* and violent contacts, notably between Eastern and Western civilizations (Roy 1938: 150).

One may note that Roy did not bring in any Hindu religious connotation to this method. For him, the Indian way of reaching the universal through a sympathetic understanding of particular cultures via the practice of tolerance and love could build up a national character which would not try to shape the different peoples and cultures in a uniform pattern. In Roy's words:

> The better minds of India are now harking back to the old ideal of culture as a means of the progressive realization of the one Universal Self in all individual- and group-selves, and the consequent elevation or transformation of individual and 'national' character and conduct, through a spirit of universal love. The anthropological attitude, while duly appreciating and fostering the varied self-expression of the Universal Spirit in different communities and countries, and not by any means seeking to mould them all in one universal racial or cultural pattern, is expected to help forward a synthesis of the past and the present, the old and the new, the East and the West (ibid).

Sarat Chandra Roy's approach to develop a nationalist anthropology in India was not a simple theoretical exercise. One should remember that he was the first Indian who founded the second professional journal of anthropology in India named *Man in India* in 1921.[1] Roy's aim was to develop an Indian School of Anthropology. In an editorial of *Man in India* published in 1985 the then editor, Surajit Chandra Sinha, commented:

> Sarat Chandra Roy's enterprise in *Man in India* was motivated by the national needs of his times and his personal pride in nationalism. As for lines of scientific enquiry he also wanted Indian scholars to seek suggestions from Western scholars and so was adopted a policy. . . It also transpires that practically all the Western and Indian pathfinders in the anthropology of India have contributed to this journal (Sinha 1985: iv-v).

Suffice it to say that Roy was not a blind nationalist. He was open to suggestions and contributions from Western experts in the pages of *Man in India* and quite a good number of Western anthropologists had contributed their original research findings on India in this pioneering journal. Sangeeta Dasgupta's perceptive comment in this regard is useful.

> Roy's long and varied career witnessed the rise of Victorian evolutionism, then diffusionism, and the eventual displacement of these by functionalism: at different points in time he applied all these concepts to the Indian context. At the same time, as a professed Hindu and nationalist Indian, particularly in the later phases of his career, Roy sought to methodologically establish an 'Indian viewpoint' for anthropology, believing that anthropology would help in the integration of national life (Dasgupta 2007: 144).

Roy's nationalism, despite his professed Hindu background, was basically Indian. In this connection, one may recall a 1933 article written by Panchanan Mitra, who was Roy's contemporary and the first professor of anthropology in India. The article was published under the editorship of Roy in *Man in India* under the title, 'Research leads in anthropology in India'. In this article, Mitra justified not only the importance of India in cultural studies but also pointed out the relevance of Indian philosophical thinking in developing modern anthropological theory. I quote him:

> It is a far cry yet from the India of the day when it would not merely echo the modern West but would try its own methods to interpret anew the laws of nature and the predominant culture pattern of India would lead it to its time old probing of all the secrets of creation through the introspection and scientific investigation of microcosmic man (Mitra 1933: 12).

One may find a similarity in the thoughts of P. Mitra and S.C. Roy in their hopes to synthesize Indian philosophy with Western anthropology. What was 'introspection' for Mitra was 'sympathetic immersion' for Roy and neither of them invoked the idea of a 'Hindu anthropology' or seemed to believe that modern anthropological concepts were already present in the ancient Hindu period in India.

II

In this section, I would narrate in some detail the practice of nationalist anthropology by some Indian anthropologists who contributed both in the pre- and post-colonial periods. But before that I would first make a brief description of some of the outstanding scholars of early Indian anthropology who, though working during the colonial period, tried to build up a nationalist tradition of anthropology. All of the following anthropologists were born in India in the nineteenth and twentieth centuries and applied their knowledge in anthropology and sociology for the cause of the marginalised and exploited tribals and other underprivileged and deprived sections of the Indian population. Although these anthropologists were influenced by the theory and methodology of the Western anthropologists, they used the Western knowledge for the cause of the exploited tribals and marginalised communities of India and also towards the materialist exposition of Indian social reality. I present below a list of ten nationalist anthropologists who did not blindly imitate the colonial masters.

Sarat Chandra Mitra (1863-1938): S.C. Mitra was the first professor of Anthropology in the first department of Anthropology in India at the University of Calcutta in 1921(Sen Gupta 1965: 54). He was a prolific writer and published numerous research articles on folklore and social cultural anthropology. His nationalist spirit was best reflected in his writings on Indian mythology as well as his interest in introducing nature study in the school curriculum as early as 1911 (Mitra 1911: 48-64).

Sarat Chandra Roy (1871-1942): He is regarded as the father of Indian anthropology. He was a practising lawyer in Ranchi and began to do research on the society and culture of the tribes of the region not out of ethnological curiosity, administrative need or evangelical mission like the Europeans, but driven by his humanitarian passion to deliver justice to the exploited tribals. He was deeply moved by the plight of the Munda, Oraon and other tribal groups, who were subjected to continued oppression by an apathetic colonial administration and by a general contempt towards them in courts of law, as 'upper caste' Hindu lawyers had little knowledge of their customs, religions, customary laws and languages. His keen interest and sympathy for the oppressed tribals inspired him to study their culture and Roy always stood for their cause. His house at Ranchi had a set of rooms prepared for his tribal clients so that those who came from far-off villages could stay on while his case was being fought in court (Ghosh 2008).

Haran Chandra Chakladar (1874-1958): He was another Indian pioneer in the study of anthropology. Chakladar was engaged in teaching and building the first department of Anthropology in Calcutta. He was a great nationalist and left his government job and joined the Dawn Society at Calcutta which was very critical of the colonial education in India (Raychaudhuri 1958: 138-9). Chakladar studied the wretched condition of the peasants and the socio-economic background of the peasant revolt under forced indigo cultivation in colonial India (Chakladar 1905: 187-205).

Bhupendranath Datta (1880-1961): Bhupendranath was the younger brother of the famous Hindu revivalist social reformer, Swami Vivekananda. He joined the anti-British struggle and was sent to prison by the colonial government in India, and later earned an M.A. in sociology from Brown University, USA, and a Ph.D. in anthropology from the University of Hamburg in 1923. His books, *Dialectics of Hindu Ritualism* (1950) and *Studies in Indian Social Polity* (1963), though published much later, can be regarded as pioneering works on Indian society and culture from a Marxist perspective (see https://en.wikipedia.org/wiki/Bhupendranath_Datta). Datta presented his research paper on the political condition of colonial India to V.I. Lenin. Lenin gave a reply to Bhupendranath and requested him to collect data on the peasant organizations in India, which was very much appreciated by Datta (https://www.marxists.org/archive/lenin/works/1921/aug/26c.htm). His contributions have not yet been included in the curriculum in Indian anthropology nor have the critics of

Indian anthropology mentioned Datta's name in their analyses of the subject.

B.R. Ambedkar (1891-1956): Ambedkar's views on the origin of caste were also neglected in the anthropology and sociology curricula in the Indian universities and colleges. Ambedkar is still a nobody in the syllabi of anthropology in India. As early as 1916, he made a novel attempt to explain the caste system in India in a paper read before the anthropology seminar of the American anthropologist Alexander Goldenweizer (1880-1940) at Columbia University. Ambedkar was then 25 years old and a doctoral student in anthropology. The full title of his paper was 'Castes in India: Their Mechanism, Genesis and Development'. Starting from a fundamental anthropological finding of tribal clan exogamy, Ambedkar had been able to show how caste endogamy was superimposed on the former. Secondly, his exposition of caste as an extreme form of class system as early as 1916 was also exemplary and this work of Ambedkar was never mentioned or referred by the world renowned scholars on caste in India (Ambedkar 1916). Take for example, G.S. Ghurye. In his famous book *Caste and Class in India* (1957), Ghurye mentions the name of Ambedkar only once on page 226 and that too as 'the leader of the Scheduled Caste', even as he discusses at length the importance of endogamy in characterizing the caste society in India (Guha 2017a).

Panchanan Mitra (1892-1936): He was a professor of ancient Indian history, culture and anthropology during 1919-29 and 1930-36 at the University of Calcutta. He was among the first Indians to study at Yale University and conducted several anthropological expeditions in India and abroad (*Bulletin of Yale University* 1941: 295-6 & *Nature* 1936: 750). He was the head of the department of anthropology of the University of Calcutta and is mostly known for his pioneering book, *Prehistoric India*, as early as 1923 (Guha 1936: 98). This book, which was the first of its kind by any Indian scholar, showed the antiquity, richness and diversity of the culture of humankind in the Indian subcontinent long before the advent of scripts.

Mitra is still the lone Indian anthropologist who wrote a book on the history of American anthropology in 1930 (Bose 2006: 1439).

Biraja Sankar Guha (1894-1961): Guha was the founder of the Anthropological Survey of India and known to the students of anthropology only as a physical anthropologist who made a classification of the Indian population on the basis of their physical features. Very few people know that he first undertook a thoroughgoing field survey on the social tensions among the refugees of the then East Pakistan for advising the government on how to understand their problems and improve their living conditions.

K.P. Chattopadhyay (1897-1963): Chattopadhyay was not only the head of the department of anthropology at the University of Calcutta but also a lifelong fighter for civil liberties movement in West Bengal before and after the independence of India. His researches on the jute mill workers and the workers of the then Calcutta Corporation were pioneering in anthropology inasmuch as they, broke away from the colonial anthropological tradition (Roy-Burman 2000: 50-1).

Tarak Chandra Das (1898-1964): Das made a marvelous empirical study, still unparalleled in global and Indian anthropology, on the devastations caused by the Bengal famine of 1943 during the colonial period. Das was such a courageous academic that he, in his presidential address of the anthropology section of the Indian Science Congress in 1941, criticized the colonial government and the Christian missionaries for doing a lot of harm to the tribals of north-east India. He had a vision for the application of anthropology for human welfare but that was forgotten by the Indian anthropologists. The critics of Indian anthropology also did not care to look at the socially relevant and nationalist studies of T.C. Das (Guha 2011: 245-65).

Nirmal Kumar Bose (1901-1972): Bose was a versatile personality in Indian anthropology. His multifaceted interest ranged from temple architecture and prehistory to transformations in tribal life under the impact of Hinduism and modernization. He was a professor at the University of Calcutta, Director of the Anthropological Survey of India and Commissioner for Scheduled Castes and Scheduled Tribes, Government of India, and was also a dedicated social worker, a Gandhian political activist, and above all a prolific writer in Bengali and English on diverse topics in professional journals, popular magazines and newspapers (a complete bibliography containing the full references of Bengali and English articles of N.K. Bose and his short life sketch can be found in Ray 1974: 61-120). Baidyanath Saraswati viewed Nirmal Kumar Bose as the 'Gandhian anthropologist' (Sraswati 2003: 1-26) while R.S. Negi in his 7th N.K. Bose memorial lecture at Indira Gandhi National Centre for the Arts mentioned that Raj Mohan Gandhi described Bose as a 'left leaning anthropologist' (Negi 2013: 1).

III

EXAMPLES OF THE PRACTICE OF NATIONALIST ANTHROPOLOGY

In this section I would narrate five remarkable cases of the practice of nationalist anthropology by some professional anthropologists of India with some biographical materials. Our first anthropologist is Bhupendranath Datta who was a freedom fighter during the British rule in India. Even though he held no university or governmental positions in the colonial or post-colonial periods, he made remarkable contributions in the field of Indian anthropology. After Bhupendranath, I will narrate the cases of Biraja Sankar Guha, the founder director of the Anthropological Survey of India and then Kshitish Prasad Chattopadhyay, head of the department of anthropology of the University of Calcutta and his faculty colleagues, Tarak Chandra Das and Nirmal Kumar Bose.

Bhupendranath Datta

The name of Bhupendranath Datta is not found in the standard encyclopedic books of anthropology in India. For example, the name, contributions and life sketch of Bhupendranath Datta did not find a place in *Bibliographies of Eminent Indian Anthropologists (with life sketches)* by S.K. Ray published by the Anthropological Survey of India and the Indian Museum in 1974. Only lately has research attention to Bhupendranath Datta's anthropological and sociological contributions been evidenced in a professional journal of Indian anthropology. See for example, R. Mukhopadhyay, 2019, 'Dr. Bhupendranath Datta: Remembering a Great Scholar in Indian Anthropology and Sociology', *Journal of the Indian Anthropological Society*, 54: 65-73. In this article, the author did not discuss Bhupendranath Datta's contribution to Physical anthropology.

The question is, who was Bhupendranath Datta? What were his anthropological contributions? Were these contributions so insignificant that he did not merit discussion in the history of Indian anthropology?

In a valuable and unique Bengali biographical dictionary named *Samsad Bangali Charitabhidhan* (revised fifth edition 2010) published by *Sahitya Samsad*, we get a short description of the life and works of Bhupendranath Datta. He was born on 4 April 1880 in Calcutta and died on 25 December 1961 in the same city, and was the youngest brother of the famous religious and social reformer Swami Vivekananda. Bhupendranath passed the then school leaving entrance examination from Calcutta Metropolitan School and joined the Bengal Revolutionary Organization. Notably, he became editor of the famous revolutionary weekly, *Jugantar*, and was sent to rigorous imprisonment for one year by the then British government for writing against the colonial rule. After being released from the jail he went out of the country in disguise under the name of Basanta Kumar Brahmachari at Belur Math with the help of Sister Nivedita. He then reached USA and earned his undergraduate degree from New York University in 1912 and then took a master's degree in sociology from the famous

Ivy League Brown University in 1914. When the First World War began, Bhupendranath reached Germany and joined the illustrious anti-British Berlin Committee organized by the Indians in exile. He was the secretary of this organization during 1916-18. But what was most remarkable in the career of this outstanding intellectual was that, along with his revolutionary activities, he continued his study and research in sociology and anthropology on India. Bhupendranath earned his Ph.D. degree in anthropology in the year 1923, from the famous Hamburg University of Germany and a became member of German Anthropological Society and German Asiatic Society. His scholarship was not limited to his specialized area in biological anthropology in which he did his doctorate but also included sociology, history, law, philosophy, statistics and literature. He wrote books and articles in Bengali, English, German, Hindi and Iranian languages. Some of his remarkable books were *Bharater Ditiya Swadhinatar Sangram* (India's Second Independence Struggle, 1949), *Bharatiyo Samaj Padhyati* (India Social Structures, 1958), *Amar Amerikar Abhijnata* (My American Experience, 1933), *Baishnab Sahitye Samajtatta* (Sociology of Vaishnava Literatures, 1945), *Banglar Itihas* (History of Bengal, 1963), *Dialectics of Hindu Ritualism* (1950), *Hindu Law of Inheritance* (1957), *Dialectics of Land Economics of India* (1952) and *Swami Vivekananda: Patriot-Prophet—A Study* (1954).

The scholarly articles published by Bhupendranath make an impressive list. His papers were published in *Man in India*, *The Sankhya*, *Modern Review*, *Journal of the Department of Letters*, *Calcutta Review*, *Bihar Orissa Research Society Journal*, and *Anthropos*. He was the first author of a paper on 'A Note on the Foot and Stature Correlation of Certain Bengal Castes and Tribes' with P.C. Mahalanobis in *The Sankhya* in 1938.

Bhupendranath Datta was also a true political activist and a worker fighting for the cause of the Indian peasantry. He should also be regarded as one of the pioneering nationalist anthropologists in India. In 1921, Datta went to Moscow to join the Communist International founded by V.I. Lenin. Bhupendranath presented his research paper on the political condition of colonial India to Lenin. Lenin gave a reply to Datta and requested him to collect data on the peasant organizations in India. As early as the mid-1930s, he was directly involved with the peasant movements in India and was the president of the *Krishaksabha* of Bengal as well as the All-India Trade Union Congress. During this period, he joined the Quit India Movement of Mahatma Gandhi and was jailed by the British government.

Unlike present-day 'specialized' anthropologists, Bhupendranath was equally strong in the two major subfields of the subject, namely, physical anthropology and social-cultural anthropology. We find quite a good number of scientific articles in various national and international journals by Datta including *Man in India*, the second professional journal of anthropology founded by Sarat Chandra Roy in 1921. I will here briefly discuss his two remarkable articles published in *Man in India* in 1935 and 1942. The title of the 1935 article is 'Ethnological Notes on Some of the Castes of West Bengal'. It should be noted that the anthropologists of this period were mainly studying tribes rather than castes. Secondly, he looked at castes from a dynamic and changing perspective which was also new for the anthropologists of his time. The fact that the same caste could take up different appearances and functions under the influence of changing political and economic conditions were not overlooked by Bhupendranath Datta. For example, like a modern anthropologist Datta observed the Bhumij community of Bankura in the following manner:

> The word 'bhumij' means indigenous . . . The bhumij of Bankura formerly had been the ghatwals of the Raja of Vishnupur; that is to say they used to serve as his militia and to watch and defend the passes which led to the state of Vishnupur. In lieu of their service, they used to get land rent free for their maintenance and used to live well. But with the disappearance of the Vishnupur state and the expropriation of their lands by the East India Company, these people have fallen off from their position (Datta 1935a: 219).

Bhupendranath's second article in *Man in India*, entitled 'Origin and Development of Indian Social Polity' and written as early as 1942, was also significant because in that long article his proposition was that 'evolution of the society and status of the castes should be evaluated according to the economic and political condition of the state'. Accordingly, he explained that caste has no biological basis and one of the most interesting subsections of the article is, 'class struggle in ancient India', in which Datta elaborately demonstrated how the origin and transformation of the caste system took place through the myriad conflicts and struggles among the different social classes revealed in the stories of the epics of India (Datta 1942: 12-63). It is really strange that this kind of original idea on the caste system which was published in one of the oldest research journals of India was overlooked by the later day Indian anthropologists. Nirmal Kumar Bose only mentioned Bhupendranath Datta's name in his article published in *The Economic Weekly* but made no attempt to understand Datta's unique approach in Indian anthropology, which dealt with caste from a Marxist point of view (Bose 1965: 1337-40).

Datta's book, *Dialectics of Hindu Ritualism*, written in the wake of his caste article, dealt with the political economy of Hindu religious institutions. Undoubtedly, it was not only one of the early Marxist sociological expositions of the Hindu religion but it was also written with a strong nationalist perspective. The author noted in the beginning:

> This book, which began to be written when the freedom of India was in the offing, is presented to the public for perusal, when New India emerging out of her Babylonian Captivity seeks a new orientation (Datta 1950).

For Bhupendranath the study of religion was important in independent India because it was part of politics and, for the anthropologist or sociologist, it was a process through which ethnic groups evolved and so its genesis was a 'fit subject of examination of a sociological investigation' (ibid 1950: i).

It would, however, be wrong to view Bhupendranath as a rigid and dogmatic intellectual. In his next book, *Hindu Law of Inheritance (An Anthropological Study)*, published in 1957, he mentioned categorically:

> Strangely, it was found out that some of the earlier writers of Indian legal

history have based their writings on the hypotheses of Morgan and Maine. But while reading the history of the cultural evolution of India, we must not forget that the present-day anthropologists say that civilization never had a unilineal development the world over. It is even admitted by Frederick Engels that the later-day anthropologists are not accepting the dictum of Morgan. Humanity never had a stereotyped evolution in its career of advancement. This we must bear in mind when we apply ourselves to Indian history (Datta 1957: ii).

This book contains detailed discussion on the two ancient systems of law which governed inheritance in India, viz., Mitakshara and Dayabhag, from a historical perspective. The book revealed the erudition of its author on Sanskritic literature and law. It threw up a challenge to Sir Henry Maine's theory on the existence of village communities in India based on principles of communal or joint ownership of agricultural land. Suffice it to say that till today the syllabi of anthropology and sociology in Indian universities contain a heavy dose of the contributions of Maine, Morgan and Marx but ironically not a single word on the original inputs of Bhupendranath Datta on the laws of property inheritance in ancient India.

His contributions in the subfield of physical anthropology were no less remarkable. He wrote a critical review of the Western anthropologists in his 84-page article, *Races of India*, published as early as 1935 in the prestigious *Journal of the Department of Letters of the University of Calcutta*. In this article, Datta had elaborately shown how the 'diverse reports', 'opposing opinions' and 'new nomenclatures' used by different authors as regards the nature of human populations in India only 'confused the students and frightened the layman'. It is interesting to note that Datta concluded the paper by saying that different 'biotypes' did exist in India (he did not use the term 'race' here) and mentioned that a thorough scientific investigation was needed to link the affinities of the Indian populations with the outside world (Datta 1935b: 165-248).

Bhupendranath Datta wrote two books on Swami Vivekananda, one in English and the other in Bengali (Datta 1954 &

1961). The Bengali book, *Swami Vivekananda*, published in 1961, is more elaborate. This is a unique, rare and pioneering culture-personality study. In this detailed anthropo-sociological research, Bhupendranath placed Vivekananda in the socio-historical context of the nineteenth century. The essence of Bhupendranath's interpretation of Vivekananda was that the latter was not satisfied only with programmes of public welfare. According to Bhupendranath Datta, Swami Vivekananda wanted a complete transformation of the prevailing exploitative social system. In the beginning of his book, Bhupendranath's words may shock the so-called Marxists. Let me freely translate them in English as follows:

> Marxists may be surprised to know that Swamiji pursued ideas similar to Marx. They would be even more surprised to know that Swamiji had openly and frankly admitted himself to be a 'socialist'. Many will also be astonished by reading that Swamiji not only used Marx's statement, 'poor are becoming poorer, and the rich are becoming more rich' in his teachings, he predicted, too, that the 'culture of the have nots' will be the culture of the Indian people in the future New India (Datta 1961).

A dedicated revolutionary and a scholar-anthropologist like Bhupendranath Datta is still a missing hero in the history of Indian anthropology and sociology (Guha 2016b: 12-13, c, d; 2018 & 2019d). The Asiatic Society, University of Calcutta, Anthropological Survey of India and Ramkrishna Mission may take a joint initiative to republish the works of Bhupendranath Datta. The sooner the better.

Our second nationalist anthropologist is B.S. Guha. I now narrate Guha's contributions.

Biraja Sankar Guha

If one looks at the writings of the admirers and faithful recorders of the contributions of B.S. Guha, certain interesting points come to one's attention. I mention them below.

The first noteworthy point is the focus on Guha's contributions centering on racial ethnology. D.P. Sinha was one of the foremost commentators on Guha and he wrote an obituary of Guha in the *American Anthropologist*. I quote Sinha:

> Guha wrote so little that his writings elude any attempt to evaluate his contributions to anthropology. However, his preoccupation with the racial ethnology of India until his death reflects his major interest and contribution (Sinha 1963: 382-7).

It was true that, compared to Verrier Elwin or N.K. Bose, Guha wrote too little, but should that be an obstacle to evaluating his contributions? On the contrary, D.P. Mukherjee, a talented anthropologist of the next generation, made a comprehensive evaluation of B.S. Guha in his long article, 'Some Anthropological Contributions of Biraja Sankar Guha: A Study in Retrospect', published in 1996. In this article, Mukherjee divided Guha's contributions in four distinct phases of which three were on racial classification and only the last phase was labelled as 'applied ethnology—overviews and exploration', and we find very little discussion on Guha's contributions in social anthropological and policy matters (Mukherjee 1996: 35-82).

The second point regarding the discussion by the admirers of Guha on his contributions to the subject of anthropology was to show that Guha had a holistic vision of anthropology. Thus, we find R.K. Bhattacharya and Jayanta Sarkar just enumerated, in their article the different sub-areas of anthropological research planned and executed by Guha under the Anthropological Survey of India. There was hardly any analysis or interpretation of Guha's vision on the development of anthropology in India (Bhattacharya & Sarkar 1996: 1-13). R.K. Bhattacharya almost repeated the same kind of description of Guha's contributions in his second B.S. Guha Memorial Lecture entitled, 'The Holistic Approach to Anthropology: B.S. Guha's Vision of the Anthropological Survey of India', without situating Guha within the larger context of Indian anthropology. Furthermore, Bhattacharya, like D.P. Sinha and D.P. Mukherjee, also mentioned that Guha's 'preoccupation was racial ethnology of India' (Bhattacharya 2012-13: 365-71).

Under these facts and circumstances, let me quickly point out some of the interesting and crucial contributions of B.S. Guha so far overlooked by both the critics of Indian anthropology and the admirers of B.S. Guha.

I will just take up two writings of Guha. The first is a short essay entitled 'The Role of Social Sciences in Nation-Building' published in *Sociological Bulletin* in 1958. The second piece is a book titled *Studies in Social Tensions among the Refugees from Eastern Pakistan*, first published in 1954 and then in 1959 by the Government of India.

The article on the role of social sciences in India is remarkable for its contemporary relevance. In this article, Guha's major emphasis was on how to understand the nature of intergroup tension (he called it 'social tension') with the help of social sciences. He proposed quite cogently that if one cannot understand the mechanisms and anatomy of conflicts between groups having different morals, values and religious practices, then just a superficial approach towards nation-building in the name of the 'melting pot theory' (as in the USA) or the epithet of 'unity in diversity'(as in case of India) will simply fail. The role of the social sciences, not the physical or biological sciences, was thought to be crucial at this point. Both R.K. Bhattacharya and D.P. Mukherjee missed this point of Guha while evaluating his contributions. I quote Guha:

> In the United States of America where the population is extremely heterogeneous and derived from many sources, with different ethnic and cultural traditions, such tensions and conflict have become very persistent in spite of the so-called melting pot theory and the ideal of inter-group tolerance, not merely as an ethical virtue but as a political necessity (Guha 1958: 149).

In the same article, Guha expressed his displeasure in giving 'undue weightage' to the superficial differences in dress, hairstyle and food habits among Indian populations. According to him the 'process of Indianization based on the underlying unifying forces of history, traditions and common values' should have been adopted (Guha 1958: 150).

Guha viewed the study of group relationships, conflict as well as tension among the human groups as the most important area in nation-building and the social sciences according to him, had a great role to play in this mighty task. For Guha, the importance of the social sciences was the greatest in solving the problems arising out of conflict and tension and he urged that the governments should keep a substantial budgetary allocation for the social sciences towards this end.

The second sociological research of Guha, which I would discuss now, was a book which was the result of teamwork. In this book, Guha had taken up the issues he outlined in his article on the role of social sciences in nation-building. This book, titled *Studies in Social Tensions among the Refugees from Eastern Pakistan* (1959), was based on intensive fieldwork done by an interdisciplinary team of researchers. Most surprisingly, virtually no discussion, let alone evaluation, of this book had been done, either by the critics of Indian anthropology or by the admirers of Guha. Complete absence and/or inadequate treatment and even improper referencing of B.S. Guha's book on social tension characterized the literature of Indian anthropology and sociology.

For example, in his obituary of B.S. Guha, D.P. Sinha just wrote two sentences on this pioneering work. I quote Sinha:

> In his later years Guha became interested in practical problems of tribal administration and social relations. He collaborated with Gardener Murphy in the UNESCO project for the study of social tensions in India, and the records of his findings appeared recently in a *Memoir of the Anthropological Survey of India* (1959) (Sinha 1963: 384).

In their accounts on him, D.P. Mukherjee and R.K. Bhattacharya did not mention about this important work of Guha. The book entitled *Anthropology of B.S. Guha (A Centenary Tribute)*, edited by R.K. Bhattacharya and Jayanta Sarkar and published by the Anthropological Survey of India in 1996, also did not contain even a brief discussion on the book on social tension by Guha in any of its six chapters penned by different authors.

Another example of this collective erasure is Vinay Kumar Srivastava's article, 'Some Responses of Communities to Social Tensions in India', published in *Anthropos* in 2003 (Srivastava 2003: 157-65). In this article, Srivastava proposed to undertake a view 'from below' to study social tension and conflict. Studying social tensions from the viewpoint of the community was exactly the research that B.S. Guha and his multidisciplinary team of workers had done and they were the first to do it among the refugees in West Bengal as early as in the 1950s. G.S. Ghurye's work on social tension was published in 1969—ten years after the aforesaid work of Guha (Ghurye 1969).

In a recent book, *Displacement and Exile: The State-Refugee Relations in India (2016)*, written by Abhijit Dasgupta, I find a paragraph on Guha's book but that too, is not properly referenced. Dasgupta mentioned that Guha's report on the social and economic background is 'sketchy' and based on some 'independent survey reports' (Dasgupta 2016: 21). In fact, the pages 3-15 as cited by Dasgupta contained a chapter written by B.K. Chatterjee on the Jirat refugee camp and were not by B.S. Guha and the information had been collected not for any 'independent survey' but as part of the UNESCO project supervised by Guha. Dasgupta did neither mention nor discuss the general introduction written by Guha. I will now discuss Guha's arguments and analysis of the findings depicted by the authors in the different chapters of the book.

In his general introduction, Guha first justified his selection of two sample areas of refugee resettlement colonies which he finalized in consultation with Gardener Murphy who was selected by the UNESCO as consultant to the Government of India in the project to understand the underlying causes of social tension in India. Guha proceeded to put the survey in the context of the wider political scenario of the country and mentioned in unequivocal terms the evil effects of the earlier 'divide and rule' policy of the British government as well as the sectarian approach of the Muslim League government of the then Bengal, which paved the way towards 'engineered' communal riots that led to large scale displacement of Hindus from East Pakistan (Guha 1959: viii). While searching the reasons behind the evacuation of the Hindus, Guha based his arguments not on any sociological theory but on the empirical findings of his multidisciplinary team of field workers. Therefore, according to him, the loss of prestige and social status which the Hindu community previously enjoyed, and the realization of the futility of regaining it now or in the near future, was a far more potent factor in creating the feeling of frustration than the loss in the economic sphere (ibid).

In the subsequent pages of the introduction, Guha went on to analyze the data on the 'areas of tension' among the Hindu refugees which were collected by his research team members through the use of social anthropological and psychological methods. Guha here made an excellent sociological analysis by putting the areas of social tension in an hierarchical and dynamic form. For Guha, his data led him to show how the areas of tension played their respective roles and the way the affected members of the community shifted their grievance and aggression from one area of tension to another. Like a social anthropologist, Guha ventured into the variation in the social tension at the level of age, sex and socio-political context.

While providing economic or psychological explanations, he did not take recourse to either the Freudian or the Marxian models. Finally, and what was really several steps ahead of his times, Guha recommended a participatory and nationalist model for the resettlement of the refugees. For him, the social tension between the refugees and the government mainly arose owing to the fact that they were treated as 'outsiders' from the governmental side. Guha opined that the refugees should be given the responsibility of managing their own resettlement camps so that they could regain their self-respect. This was the view of Biraja Sankar Guha whom I would like to regard as one of the pioneering applied anthropologists of post-independent India (Guha 2018e: 1-12).

It is an irony that both the critics and the admirers of

Indian anthropology during the post-colonial period became more Westernized and missed the emerging spirit of a nationalist anthropology in the writings of B.S. Guha.

Finally, it may be said that writing on the contributions of the pioneers of Indian anthropology should be placed in the wider context of the already existing critiques of the discipline. Without this broader framework, mere reporting and some technical discussion on the contributions of any anthropologist may not yield insights in the historiography of Indian anthropology. Accordingly, I have situated the sociological/social anthropological contributions of B.S. Guha in the context of the critiques of Indian anthropology, which seemed to me to be rather misplaced as far as the contributions of the Indian pioneers, here in this case Biraja Sankar Guha, were concerned.

The third anthropologist in my list is K.P. Chattopadhyay. Let me describe his nationalist contributions in the context of his life and works.

Kshitish Prasad Chattopadhyay

Kshitish Prasad Chattopadhyay was one of most distinguished anthropologists of India. He was born on 15 December 1897 and had a brilliant academic career. Chattopadhyay was a descendent of two great social reformers of nineteenth century Bengal, namely, Raja Ram Mohan Roy and Pandit Ishwar Chandra Vidyasagar and he was an affine of the famous family of Rabindranath Tagore. He was educated in the Metropolitan School in Kolkata and then in Vidyasagar and Presidency Colleges of the University of Calcutta in Physics. Kshitish Prasad ranked seventh in matriculation in 1913 and stood first in his I. Sc. examination in 1917. He earned a first-class honours degree in physics from the University of Calcutta. Chattopadhyay was a student of the famous Indian scientists like Meghnad Saha, Satyen Bose and Acharya Prafulla Chandra Roy. Thereafter, he worked as a research student of C.V. Raman.

In 1919, he went to the United Kingdom and took his admission at Cambridge University in physics and began his studies under famous physicists like J.J.Thompson and E. Rutherford. But soon he changed his subject and obtained his master's degree in anthropology in 1922. He came in contact with the famous British anthropologist W.H.R. Rivers, who was his teacher. Chattopadhyay was awarded the Anthony Wilkins Fellowship to carry out his research on the Newar community of Nepal. The fellowship was later withdrawn because of his activities with the Indian Seamen's Union (London), which were regarded as objectionable and he was not allowed to visit Nepal for his fieldwork by the then colonial government (Hutton 1963: 155-6). He came back to India in 1922 with M.A. degree in anthropology from Cambridge University (IJCS 1964: 111-12).

After his return to India, Chattopadhyay joined as a lecturer in anthropology at the University of Calcutta in 1923 but within a short period of time left the university and inspired by C.R. Das and Subhas Chandra Bose, who were leaders of the Congress party then running the civic body joined as an education officer of the Corporation of Calcutta. He worked there during 1924-37 and trained 1,500 primary school teachers to impart free education to children. In 1924, there were very few primary schools under the Calcutta Corporation. K.P. Chattopadhyay took special initiatives to establish more primary schools and before he left the job 232 primary schools had come up in which more than 50,000 children belonging to the poor families were being educated. Chattopadhyay also wrote two primers in Bengali named *Lekhapada*, using the most advanced teaching methods.[2] While working at Calcutta Corporation, he actively participated in the Civil Disobedience Movement of Mahatma Gandhi. In 1937 he rejoined the University of Calcutta as head and professor of the department of anthropology where he worked, until his retirement in 1962 (Béteille 1994: xi). Notably, Chattopadhyay was a lifelong fighter for civil liberties movement in West Bengal before and after the independence of India. His research studies on the jute mill workers and the workers of the then Calcutta Corporation were pioneering in the subject and they broke away from the colonial anthropological tradition.[3] Chattopadhyay's range of interest in anthropology was extremely varied and he was a prolific writer with sound command in statistical sciences as well as in Sanskrit. He wrote more than a hundred scientific articles in English and also popularized anthropological themes in the vernacular. His posthumous book, *Ancient Indian Culture Contacts and Migrations*, was published by Sanskrit College of Calcutta in 1965 and it was reviewed with admiration by C. von Furer Haimendorf in the *Bulletin of the School of Oriental and African Studies*, London in 1968 (vol. 31, issue 2, pp. 450-1).[4] The articles he wrote were published in many international and national level professional journals, like *Man*, *American Journal of Physical Anthropology*, *Ethnos*, *Journal of the Royal Asiatic Society of Bengal*, *International Journal of Comparative Sociology*, *Sankhya*, *Man in India* and *Modern Review*. They were on theoretical and core areas of anthropology like anthropometry, material culture, kinship, marriage, social organization and inheritance of property as well as on applied areas namely, culture contact, culture change, personality and culture, social conflict, tribal development, rehabilitation, education and national planning. He most intensively studied the Santals of Bengal and his *Report on the Santals* was published by the University of Calcutta in 1947. Apart from Santals, he also conducted studies on the social organization of the Khasi and Korku. The influence of W.H.R. Rivers on Chattopadhyay's works on kinship study was evident but he was also critical of the applicability of several Western anthropological categories, which he found inadequate for the interpretation of Indian reality. Rajatsubhra Mukhopadhyay succinctly observed that K.P. Chattopadhyay could not find any advantage in the use of the term 'nuclear family' since it did not play any role comparable to the nucleus of a cell in the Indian context. He also strongly suggested treating 'joint' and 'extended' family types as structurally and organizationally two different types of social institutions in the Indian situation (Mukhopadhyay 2000: 39-49).

Although his major area of interest was in kinship, family and marriage in tribal societies, Chattopadhyay was not confined to either in these areas or among the tribal populations only. As early as 1923, he wrote an article on the history of Newar culture in Nepal in which he combined historical data with contemporary social practices to show the past continuity of the Newar caste system and social divisions down to the present time. In the same vein, his three important papers on the history of Indian social organization (1935), social organization of Satkarnis and Sungas (1927) and Dharma worship (1942) were attempts to explain some ancient institutions and customs with the help of social anthropological methods of inquiry. Another area of Chattopadhyay's interest was the study of the material culture of the tribal and non-tribal populations, and he published quite a number of articles and abstracts on this important topic in anthropology. He wrote on Korku house types, the plough and the clod crusher, the Bondo and Korku tree-press, Santal fish-traps and bird nets, Bengal coiled basketry, Indian rafts, the toe-peg sandals of India and Korku dress and ornaments.

N.C. Choudhury, a former director of the Anthropological Survey of India and one of the illustrious students of K.P. Chattopadhyay, perceptively noted that, during the 1950s, Chattopadhyay shifted his interest to social and material changes in traditional cultures, which started with his 1949 *Man in India* article on changes in the Santal economy (Choudhury 2000: 52-9). In this period, he wrote on the culture contact and changes in the Vedic age (1955), studied changes in traditional cultures (1957), sari border changes (1957), changes in Santal songs (1957), some changes in Khasi culture (1960), and structural changes in family in Bengal (1959). The paper on sari border changes is quite unique. In this paper Chattopadhyay had shown how the introduction of mill made saris (a piece of long cloth worn by Indian women) gave an upper hand to the *mahajans* (money-lenders who loaned money at much higher rates than banks) which forced the traditional weavers of Bengal to adopt new designs and ultimately made the latter dependent upon the former and turned them into wage labourers (Chattopadhyay 1957: 95-9).

An unorthodox kind of study undertaken by K.P. Chattopadhyay and his co-workers dealt with the problems and living conditions of undergraduate students at the University of Calcutta. During the early 1950s, Chattopadhyay, in collaboration with the statistics department of the University of Calcutta, conducted a survey on the living conditions of the undergraduate students and the report of this pioneering survey was published by the university in 1954. Another study, jointly conducted by K.P. Chattopadhyay and P. Bose of the department of statistics, dealt with how the guardians planned education for their children and this study was also published by the University of Calcutta in 1962. Both these application-oriented empirical surveys were not only unusual at the time but are still very rare in Indian anthropology and other social sciences. With these studies, K.P. Chattopadhyay laid the foundation of educational anthropology in India, which has not yet come to fruition in Indian anthropology.

One of Chattopadhyay's most remarkable contribution beyond anthropology was on the rehabilitation of the people affected by the Great Bengal Famine of 1943 in which he collaborated with the famous statistician P.C. Mahalanobis to work out a plan for successful rehabilitation of the famine-affected families of undivided Bengal. The jointly authored book, *Famine and Rehabilitation in Bengal* (1946) by P.C. Mahalanobis and K.P. Chattopadhyay is still regarded as one of the best known early applied researches on the subject. Two other remarkable applied social anthropological research studies by Chattopadhyay were on municipal labour in Calcutta (done jointly with G.S. Roy in 1947) and a socio-economic survey of the jute mill workers of Bengal in 1952 which were published by the University of Calcutta. Chattopadhyay developed an early interest in the study of caste and class in Bengal villages. His two unpublished papers read at Gokhale Institute, Pune, on changing values and social patterns in caste society in West Bengal villages (1961) and class relations in Bengal villages (1962) along with a conference paper in Calcutta bear testimony to this fact.

Chattopadhyay's knowledge and interest in the application of statistics in anthropology were also pioneering. As early as 1941, he published an article entitled, 'Application of Statistical Methods to Anthropological Research', in the famous journal *Sankhyâ: The Indian Journal of Statistics* edited by P.C. Mahalanobis. In this article, Chattopadhyay discussed the problems of sampling in physical and social anthropology with the help of simple examples. In this paper, he also cautioned anthropologists about the importance of considering environmental and historical factors while collecting data and/or defining their populations and societies. In 1951, he wrote another interesting methodological paper entitled, 'The racial composition of Bengalees', which was published in a supplementary volume of Census of India 1951 edited by A. Mitra titled, *The Tribes and Castes of West Bengal.* In this article, he dealt with the differences of the same anthropometric measurements recorded by physical anthropologists on similar population groups. He criticized H.H. Risley's measurements, which 'suffered from a serious defect in that his assistant was not properly trained' according to Chattopadhyay, Risley did not carry out any cross-check 'regarding the comparability of measurements taken'. Another area of Chattopadhyay's interest was social psychology. Chattopadhyay wrote articles in the *Indian Journal of Psychology* on temporary loss of memory (1939) and personality and culture (1957) as well as on juvenile delinquency in Calcutta in the *International Journal of Comparative Sociology* (1962).

K.P. Chattopadhyay represented India at the international conferences of the anthropologists held in London, Vienna and Paris in 1934, 1952 and 1960, respectively. He delivered the keynote address at the international seminar on the problems of juvenile delinquency in London organised by UNESCO in 1960 and the lecture was published in 1962 in the prestigious *International Journal of Comparative Sociology* (vol. 3, no. 2, pp. 221-8). Chattopadhyay was a Fellow of the National Institute of Sciences of India and Honorary Fellow of the famous Sanskrit College of Calcutta. He was actively engaged with the Asiatic Society of Bengal and served as the anthropological secretary of this renowned institute.

During 1937-62, K.P. Chattopadhyay served as the head of the department of anthropology at the University of Calcutta which was in its formative phase. During this period, the department flourished in all the three major subdisciplines of anthropology namely, physical anthropology, prehistoric archaeology and social-cultural anthropology. In 1955, the department of anthropology at the University of Calcutta was chosen by the university and the UNESCO to hold a conference on the 'study of changes in traditional culture' and, with the able academic and administrative leadership of Chattopadhyay, it was not only held most successfully but the whole proceedings along with the discussions were also meticulously recorded and published in the form of a book by the University of Calcutta in 1957. Under the encouraging guidance of Chattopadhyay, many of his students and teachers won national and international recognition. Some of his students who later became famous in the national and international arenas were Ramkrishna Mukherjee, Surajit Sinha, B.K. Roy Burman, André Béteille and others.

K.P. Chattopadhyay was an anthropologist with a nationalist and humanist spirit who dedicated himself to the welfare of humanity. In an obituary of Chattopadhyay, which was published in *Man* (vol. 53, nos. 193, 194; 1963, pp. 155-6) the eminent anthropologist, J.H. Hutton, noted:

> Apart from his academic work, he was always active in promoting the welfare of his fellow men. As a student in England, he had worked among seamen in the East End of London; in India the free primary education system in Calcutta was largely his work, as treasurer of the People's Relief Committee, famine relief and rehabilitation work in the rural areas of Bengal owed much to him, and during

the communal riots of 1946 he organized a 'Peace Corps' to restore order.

K.P. Chattopadhyay remained active after his retirement from the University of Calcutta. Just before his fatal cerebral thrombosis in May 1963 he had been working on his book on the Santals and a volume on the culture contact and migration in ancient India, which was published in 1965. Chattopadhyay passed away on 31 May 1963 in Calcutta.

The fourth nationalist anthropologist in my list is Tarak Chandra Das.

Tarak Chandra Das

Tarak Chandra Das was born in January 1898 in erstwhile undivided Bengal now Bangladesh. Nothing in detail is known about his family background and school education in the existing literature. He had his early education in Tangail and Rajshahi of present Bangladesh. Das obtained his M.A. degree in ancient Indian history and culture from the University of Calcutta. He joined the newly-founded department of anthropology at Calcutta University in 1921 as a research scholar and then he became lecturer in 1923. He finally retired in the rank of reader from the department in 1963 (Ray 1974: 56-60).

One comprehensive available account of the list of publications of T.C. Das, including a short life-sketch, was prepared by the reference librarian in the Central Library of the Anthropological Survey of India, Shyamal Kumar Ray, in his invaluable book, *Bibliographies of Eminent Indian Anthropologists (with Life Sketches)*, published by the Anthropological Survey of India and Indian Museum in July 1974. The volume contains the list of publications and short life sketches of 12 eminent Indian anthropologists including Tarak Chandra Das. The compilation begins with L.K. Ananthakrishna Iyer (1861-1937) and S.S. Sarkar (1908-69) is the last anthropologist covering a span of more than one hundred years if we take the year of birth of Iyer and the year of death of Sarkar as the two ends of the continuum. T.C. Das falls almost in the middle of the continuum.

The bibliographical records of T.C. Das showed that he had altogether 40 publications, that is, almost one in every year of his academic career. He published 31 full-length articles, 2 books, 6 abstracts, 2 jointly authored books and 1 joint article. The national and international journals in which he published were prestigious and included *Man*, *Anthropos*, *Ethnos*, *Man in India*, *Calcutta Review*, *Modern Review*, *Sociological Bulletin*, *Journal of Social Research*, *Journal of the Department of Letters* and *Anthropological Papers* of the University of Calcutta. Apart from kinship and social organization, his areas of research interest displayed remarkable diversity which ranged between sun worship (1924), fish in Bengali culture (1931-2), the disposal of dead among the tribals (1940), improvement of museums (1943), scheme for tribal welfare, impact of industrialization on peasantry (1960), and an anthropological analysis of the Bengal dowry restriction bill (1941).

Tarak Chandra Das became internationally famous for his ethnography on the Purum Kukis of north-east India. His brilliant monograph, *The Purums: An Old Kuki Tribe of Manipur*, published in 1945 by the Calcutta University, became one of the major data resources in the acrimonious debate on descent versus alliance theories on kinship in Anglo-American anthropology which involved mavericks like Claude Levi-Strauss, George Homans, David Schneider, Rodney Needham, Floyd Lounsbury and others. The Indian anthropologists too, continued their ethnographic enterprise on the Purum on behalf of the premier governmental institution of the country—the Anthropological Survey of India. A team of anthropologists were sent to the field area where Das conducted his ethnographic observations during 1931-6 and a book was published entitled, *Proceedings of the Symposium on Purum (Chote) Revisited* in 1985, as an outcome of a symposium in which about 20 anthropologists and two educated members of the tribe participated and presented their views/papers. In the first volume of his book, *Rise of Anthropology in India*, L.P. Vidyarthi described in detail the findings of Das in the different chapters of the monograph with much admiration for his meticulousness and penetrating analyses. In the final section of his description, Vidyarthi discussed the suggestions advanced by Das for the betterment of the Purums. According to Vidyarthi, with the publication of the Purum book, T.C. Das 'set an example of a systematic presentation of ethnographic data' (ibid 1978: 80). He concluded the discussion on Das's monograph with the following comment:

> His monograph, though not well-known to Indian scholars, remains a piece of meticulous fieldwork and penetrative analysis. It will continue to serve as a model for ethnographic research in anthropology (Vidyarthi I: 81).

In the concluding chapter of the Purum book, Das elaborated on the dynamic nature of Purum society which had undergone changes through historical times and also on the different aspects of Purum culture under various kinds of external influences. Secondly, Das was keenly interested to understand the nature of the 'productive system' (he did not use the Marxian term, *means of production*, but it was clear that by the term, 'productive system', he did not only refer to technology and material culture but also to the economy and society) in a dynamic rather than in a functional framework. Thirdly, without mechanically borrowing terms from the Western Marxist scholars, Das made a very sincere empirical attempt to record the processes by which the new productive system, characterized by the plough and plains-land cultivation had begun to influence the different sectors of the Purum society, viz., inheritance, marriage and religion. Apart from looking into the internal socio-cultural changes brought about by the adoption of the plough cultivation among the Purums, Das was also aware of the wider politico-economic forces which were at work in the region inhabited by this community.

Another related significant work of Das remained unnoticed

by Indian scholars. This work was published in the prestigious international journal, *Anthropos*, as early as 1937 under the title 'Some Notes on the Economic and Agricultural Life of a Little-Known Tribe on the Eastern Frontier of India' (Das 1937: 440-9). In this paper Das dealt with the relationship between the variation in technology of agricultural practices with the natural environment and the socioeconomic consequences of this variation within the same tribe. The name of the tribe is Chiru who, like the Purums, belonged to the old Kuki group of tribes of north-east India. A careful reading of the paper revealed that the economic life of the Chirus which Das constructed, was not a simple description of the methods of shifting hill cultivation and the associated religious rituals and rites. Neither was it an ethnographic report for the search of borrowed culture traits from the neighbouring tribes and Hinduized populations nor was it an attempt to locate the Chirus in the classical scheme of social evolution. The ethnography of Das, on the other hand, is a penetrating analysis of the various socio-cultural dimensions of shifting hill cultivation in an environmental framework and slow changes that had been taking place at the time of his field observation. It is interesting to note that one of the earliest publications of Julian Steward, in which he dealt with the relationship between productive technology and the other sectors of culture, was published in *Anthropos* the same year (Steward 1937: 87-104). If one compares the paper of Steward with that of Das, then certain important similarities become evident. Like T.C. Das, Julian Steward also placed emphasis on the importance of the environment and the economy in shaping the social organizational features of a culture.

T.C. Das' book on the 1943 famine of Bengal was a unique and rare first-hand study done by any anthropologist or social scientist on the victims of one of the greatest tragedies of our country occurring under colonial rule. The book, entitled *Bengal Famine (1943): As Revealed in a Survey of the Destitutes of Calcutta*, was published by the University of Calcutta in 1949. An earlier version of the book was discussed in the then

British Parliament and some of the recommendations advanced by Das were adopted by the Famine Inquiry Commission in 1944 formed by the colonial government for the prevention of future famines in India. Pandit Jawaharlal Nehru in his book, *The Discovery of India*, also mentioned about the anthropological survey conducted by Das on the famine-affected population of Bengal and expressed his confidence in the results of the survey in contrast to the one carried out by the government. Much later, the Nobel laureate economist, Amartya Sen, and a renowned social historian, Paul Greenough, have used Das' original work in their books on the famine (Sen 1999 & Greenough 1982). Still later, an American historian, Mark Tauger, who debated with Sen and Greenough on the Bengal famine, had to depend on Das' book for the holistic approach undertaken by the latter in understanding the causes of the famine (Tauger 2009: 166-96). Of all the works of T.C. Das, *Bengal Famine* can be regarded as the most valuable and unique contribution for the following reasons. The field-based study of the Bengal famine of 1943 which was conducted by T.C. Das is not a typical anthropological study of a tribe or a caste village. Let us enumerate the facts.

First, this is the only first-hand study done by a team of trained anthropologists on the Bengal famine.

Second, the book which was written by Das has not received any attention by successive generation of anthropologists and sociologists in India.

Third, in this study, Das and his teammates employed traditional anthropological methods (e.g. genealogy, case history, participant observation) for the collection of data not from a specific tribe or caste in a rural setting, but from a scattered and heterogeneous group of human beings displaced from the different districts of undivided Bengal and affected by the acute food shortage.

Fourth, the field work and survey on the famine-affected population were carried out mainly in the city of Calcutta.

Fifth, the report and the recommendations based on the anthropological study of the famine in Bengal were taken into consideration by the policymakers and administrators at the highest level of governance.

Sixth, the explanation provided by Das on the causes of Bengal famine surpassed the prevalent anthropological interpretations of social events.

Taken together, the above facts have made *Bengal Famine* an unorthodox kind of anthropological study even by modern standards.

The anthropological odyssey of T.C. Das, like many of his contemporaries, began with observations on tribal social structure, economic organization, material culture and religion, but he gradually focused his findings towards application and policy oriented arguments in a macro-framework. Das was not only a meticulous ethnographer but, during the middle part of his career, also ventured into territories which did not come under the tradition of anthropology developed in India under Western influence. The study of the Great Bengal famine is the finest example of this genre.

Apart from his success as an ethnographer, Das was also an armchair anthropologist. His studies on the culture around fish in Bengal, museums and dowry restriction law provided examples of his keen interest in dealing with archival materials and written texts in social anthropological and sociological studies on Indian problems.

Besides the study of Bengal famine, there were other notable and almost unknown studies made by Das on subjects of national importance and which were rarely taken up seriously by the Indian and foreign anthropologists. One such study by Das was on the Bengal dowry restriction bill and the other was on the Hindu code bill. The third paper was on museums. The first two papers were published in *The Modern Review* and *The Calcutta Review* in 1941 and 1944, respectively, and the third was published in *The Calcutta Review* in 1943. In the first two papers, Das argued in favour of conducting proper sociological studies before introducing new legislations which, in his opinion, might have caused unwanted effects in these intricate and complex social matters. The third article, entitled 'Practical Steps Towards the Improvements of Museums in India' (1943), was unique because, in this article, Das developed the idea of building 'Economic Museums' in which anthropologists and other scientists would work for the economic development of the people in independent India.

In the later part of his career, Das took up the study of tribal societies in India beyond simple ethnography. His three papers on the scheme for tribal welfare (1960), social change in tribal society (1962), and tribal culture under modern impact (1963) are the best examples of the aforementioned trend (Guha 2016a). In all these articles, Das used his massive ethnographic experience to understand the changes that had been taking place among the tribes of eastern India and attempted to formulate general policies towards their development. His ideas about tribal development were pragmatic and he never believed in the policy of isolating tribals from the mainstream of Indian culture. Das gave top priority to the spread of primary and vocational education among the tribals and wanted them to be economically self-sufficient. In all these publications, Das strongly advocated the positive role anthropologists could play in tribal development of the newly independent country. But at the same time, he was well aware of the limitations of anthropology in this regard. For example, in the article, 'A scheme for tribal welfare', he cautioned:

> The stock of our knowledge about the tribal people of India is very limited. We have about two scores of books on tribal ethnography of India. Many of these books written at a time when the subject itself had not attained its present methodological efficiency are not serviceable to the applied anthropologist. Most of these books do not deal with the economic condition of the tribes in proper detail. As a result, the information available from this source are of little value to the state or to the social worker (Das 1960: 107).

Das envisaged that every state in India having one lakh or more tribal population should set up an independent institution for tribal survey and research for the purpose of the application of anthropological knowledge towards tribal development. These research institutions, according to Das, were to be financed by the government but kept outside its control, since they would be the ones to take up evaluation of various welfare schemes executed by the various government departments. They should be handed over to local universities having anthropology and sociology departments (ibid).

In 1941, Das delivered the presidential address in the anthropology section of the Indian Science Congress. The lecture was a 28-page full-length paper entitled 'Cultural Anthropology in the Service of the Individual and the Nation'. This paper can be regarded as one of the pioneering articles on applied anthropology in India written in a truly nationalist spirit. In the address, Das elaborately charted out the future path of Indian anthropology with a rich description of the social dynamics of the tribal and peasant societies in India in the context of the role of anthropologists in nation-building[5] (Das 1941: 1-28).

T.C. Das was a brilliant teacher in the formative years of Indian anthropology at the University of Calcutta and his meticulous training in ethnographic field work was well-known. Famous anthropologists like Ramkrishna Mukherjee, Surajit Sinha, B.K. Roy Burman, Ajit Danda, André Béteille, Prabodh Bhowmick and Amal Kumar Das were trained by this unsung hero of Indian anthropology who passed away on 26 July 1964.

Nirmal Kumar Bose

The fifth nationalist anthropologist in the list is Nirmal Kumar Bose.

The case of Bose as an anthropologist and a nationalist freedom fighter present a contradiction to any scholar seriously interested in the history of anthropology in India. Bose was definitely a nationalist as observed by the renowned scholars but his specific anthropological account on the assimilation of the tribes into the caste system had serious limitations.

Nirmal Kumar Bose was a Gandhian nationalist unlike his predecessor Sarat Chandra Roy and contemporary Tarak

Chandra Das. The anthropologist successors of Bose, like Surajit Chandra Sinha and André Béteille missed this contradiction in Bose's personality. The real challenges like famine, partition and development caused displacement encountered by the people and the policy makers of the new nation in the post-colonial period did not find an important place in the anthropology of this great anthropologist of India, although Bose was a committed social worker and non-violent political activist dedicated towards the upliftment of the untouchable castes and maintenance of communal harmony.

At the end of his career Bose advocated the crucial importance of the application of anthropology in solving the problems of nation building and here lies the historical significance of re-evaluating the works of the other pioneering anthropologists of India who made solid and inspiring contributions toward nation building in the newly independent country. I have just made this humble assessment to place Nirmal Kumar Bose within his anthropological milieu without making any attempt to dwarf this towering personality in Indian anthropology.

Although, Bose did not write on the notable contributions of anthropologists in dealing with the challenges of nation building in independent India, his own works at the Anthropological Survey of India bear testimony to putting anthropology towards the service of the nation. His position was in order to contribute towards nation building one has to know the country first and one should realise that the greater part of our country lived in the villages. Just after joining the Anthropological Survey of India in 1959 as Director Bose involved all researchers in a mega project to collect data on the socio-economic and cultural aspects of villages covering 311 districts of India out of 322 and the results of this survey was published in a volume entitled *Peasant Life in India: A Study in Indian Unity and Diversity* in 1961 (Bose 1961). The plethora of data on the material and ideological aspects of rural India contained in the book is one of the best works done by the anthropologists in the government department. This is a book which has tremendous contemporary policy relevance at least for three important reasons. First this book revealed with empirical information that peasant life in India cannot be improved without understanding its material diversity. Second, it showed the real value of collecting first hand information from the peasants, which should be the guiding principle behind planning and policy formulation from below, not from the top. Third, peasant life in India has an underlying cultural unity of non-competitive tolerance and peaceful coexistence, which shaped the ambition and aspiration of the peasants throughout the centuries. Can we forget these three lessons even today when we frame our policies towards the development of rural India?

I will now take up N.K. Bose's famous report on the problems of North-East India, which he wrote as the Commissioner for Scheduled Castes and Scheduled Tribes published in 1968-9. After reviewing the situation in the northeast as an anthropologist as well as a policymaker Bose lucidly formulated the governmental policy for the newly independent nation, which was summarised by Surajit Sinha in his 1st N.K. Bose memorial lecture delivered at Indira Gandhi National Centre for the Arts (IGNCA) in 1993. I quote from Sinha's paper:

(a) The main emphasis should be on building up an economy of unexploitative interdependence between the hills and the plains.
(b) The cultural policy should be extremely permissive and tolerant, providing facilities for autonomous development from the home base of specific tribes or related cluster of tribes.
(c) Demand for cessation should not be negotiable and this should be firmly and unequivocally communicated to those leaders who may be involved in such anti-national demands (Sinha 1993: 15).

According to Surajit Sinha,

... this is perhaps the clearest and most sensible overall policy guideline which has been so far formulated about the unique mountainous tribal regions located at the international frontier of Northeast India (ibid.).

I would go further and do not hesitate to say that the situation in the northeast of our country since Bose's formulation of the aforementioned policy guidelines has not improved but that does not mean that those guidelines have lost their relevance today. With the entry of the cash economy and rapid destruction of forests and the increasing pressure of population both in the hills and the plains the economic inequality between the hills and the plains have increased and the anti-national activities are also on the rise. Have we been able to formulate any new policy after Nirmal Kumar Bose? Should we not relook at those policy guidelines of Bose in dealing with the problems of Northeast India?

I would now come to Bose's shining idea about tribal welfare in the context of the ground realities of independent India. In his sectional Chairman's speech delivered at the Third Annual Session of the Indian Conference of Social Work on 5 December 1953 Bose did not hesitate to criticise the higher caste Hindu view of assigning a low status to the Adibasis, which resulted in the conversion of the latter to Christianity in many places and thereby gave rise to anti-national and separatist attitudes. In the same article, Bose also expressed his scepticism towards the governmental approach of merely giving economic and educational benefits to the tribals. He stated

> The best course would be to try and build up a caste-free new India, where no occupation is high and none low, and this with the help of those who are within the caste organization as well as those who stand outside it (Bose 1953: 218).

Bose with his characteristic way of explaining complex problems in a simple and straight forward manner questioned the colonial mentality towards the management forests in the abovementioned lecture article, which is relevant till today,

> In the hills of Orissa, there lives a a tribe known as the Kharias. There is another who are known as the 'Monkey-eating Kols' or Birhors. These tribes live by collecting honey and wax or the manufacture of ropes, and by selling them to the agricultural population who, live near by. The members of these tribes have no fear of the jungle; they live in the jungle, and are trained to take care of themselves even when they wander for days on end in the forest territory. In India we have large forests, and

men have to be employed in taking care of those forests. Why should we not take advantage of the acquired aptitudes of these Birhors and Kharias; and instead of driving them into the position of settled cultivators living in a crowded environment, why can we not recruit our foresters from among those who are in love with the forests? (Bose 1953: 218).

It is true that Nirmal Kumar Bose being a great visionary of Indian anthropology, who held important governmental and university positions in post-independent India and was a personal secretary to M.K. Gandhi did not narrate the specific contributions and role of anthropologists on nation building in independent India in his two important books entitled *Problems of National Integration* (1967) and *Problems of Indian Nationalism* (1969) but in these books he treated nation building from a brave perspective. For example, in the second book, which was originally a lecture delivered by Bose in the A.N. Sinha Institute of Social Studies at Patna, he spoke unequivocally against all kinds of separatist tendencies which was growing in the country. Bose was of the opinion that the greatest danger of nation building lurks behind our policy of reservation. I quote Bose:

....[T]he administrative machinery of many of our States will have to be reformed so that men of all States can function with freedom and equality anywhere in India in order to render the best services possible to the 'masses', in Gandhi's sense of the term. The present concern for somehow securing maximum benefits to the 'Sons of the Soil' (sometimes nicknamed as the sos) and their protection from open competition, must be replaced before we can turn the corner. Those who are backward may be given every facility for education, if they have been denied this on account of social suppression or poverty in the past. But while seeking employment they must be encouraged, not to seek protection but face competition in the open market (Bose 1969: 41).

Bose viewed the problems of nation building in a critical and constructive manner. While admitting the failures of Five Year Plans he recognised the fact that the shortcomings had also been realised by the planners and he came forward with his warnings and suggestions. While welcoming the government's decision to entrust the community development programmes to locally elected bodies, he cautioned that these bodies might also be successful in manipulating the local organisations to remain entrenched in power (Bose 1967: 71-2). What then is the remedy? A committed follower of Gandhi and an anthropologist influenced by British and American anthropology, Bose at the end of his book *Problems of National Integration* did not hesitate to state his recommendation towards nation building by duly acknowledging the Russian revolutionary Leon Trotsky:

> The supreme task is to turn the country's mind to the promotion of the interests of those who toil and produce the nation's wealth. All others can and should exist if they subserve the interests of the toiling millions. And the beginnings of this adventure will lie in little things well done, rather than in great things done in an inefficient manner (Bose 1967: 73).

IV

In this section, I will narrate the anthropological contributions of B.R. Ambedkar which not only differed markedly from the views of anthropologists like N.K. Bose but may also be viewed from a nationalist perspective. The inclusion of Ambedkar in my list of nationalist anthropologists in India, therefore, is neither arbitrary nor accidental. B.R. Ambedkar's book entitled *The Untouchables* published as early as 1948 is a remarkable example of anthropological and historical scholarship on the origin and the present social condition of one of the most underprivileged sections of the Indian society (Ambedkar 1948). Furthermore, this great thinker of India provided a comprehensive future plan for nation building through industrialisation and agrarian revolution having immense contemporary relevance (Kumar 2020: 37-56). It is a fact of history that Dr B.R. Ambedkar was not only one of the most important architects of the secular Constitution of independent India but also had his early higher educational training in anthropology at Columbia University in the United States of America in the milieu of Franz Boas and his famous students like Alexander Goldenweizer and Ruth Benedict. Ambedkar was influenced by Boas' work which demystified the then ethnocentric bias of the racial superiority and Semitism propagated by some of the scientists and scholars in America and Nazi Germany. In a recent article published in 2018 in the *Journal of South Asia Studies*, Jesús F. Cháirez-Garza has argued that during his study at Columbia University in 1913-16, Ambedkar was exposed to the ideas of Franz Boas on race and culture.[6] Boas demonstrated that race had no biological basis and this influenced Ambedkar to refute the claims of the proponents of the theory of the biological basis of the origin of caste system in India. In the words of Cháirez-Garza:

> . . . During his time as a student at Columbia, Ambedkar familiarised himself with ideas that rejected the fixity of identities, societies and racial hierarchies . . . Ambedkar, at different stages in his career, put into practice similar concepts to the ones used by Boas to condemn the practice of Untouchability. In other words, Ambedkar rejected the idea that the identity and place in society of Untouchables was determined by their supposed racial inferiority. Instead, Ambedkar emphasised the importance of culture, which in Boas' vision, included the environment, psychology and language. These elements were key in the construction of identities and societies. Ambedkar adopted this mode of thinking to argue that Untouchability was not fixed or hereditary. It was a cultural problem that could be fought and eradicated (Cháirez-Garza 2018: 4).

Interestingly, Cháirez-Garza noted in his article that Ambedkar was not a blind follower of Boas but his contributions, though unnoticed by the doyens of Indian anthropology, have a continuing influence. I quote from the above article:

> . . . Ambedkar did not follow blindly the work of Boas. Rather, he transformed it to suit his political and ideological battles against Untouchability. In so doing, Ambedkar made similar arguments to prominent Western academics, such as Ruth Benedict and Alexander Lesser. It is important to note that Ambedkar's connections with anthropology do not end there. Just to mention a few examples, in his seminal work, *The Interpretation of Cultures*, Clifford Geertz draws several times from Ambedkar's concept of nationalism as a 'feeling of a corporate sentiment of oneness'. In the same way, in his *Homo Hierarchicus*, Louis Dumont, without acknowledging Ambedkar, defines caste as a state of mind (ibid: 26-7).

As early as 1916, Ambedkar with his understanding enriched by Boasian anthropological thought, made a novel attempt to explain the caste system in India in a paper read before the anthropology seminar of Alexander Goldenweizer (1880-1940) at Columbia University. Ambedkar was then 25 years old and a doctoral student in anthropology. The full title of his paper was 'Castes in India: Their Mechanism, Genesis and Development'. It was an 18-page document which contained a pure and detached academic exercise on the nature of the caste system in India. Nowhere in the paper have we found any comment or observation from the personal experiences of the author. It was full of critical scholarship on the then existing anthropological and sociological literature on caste in a lucid and argumentative fashion. In the first part of the paper, Ambedkar dealt with the works of four famous scholars like Emile Senart (1847-1928), John Nesfield (1836-1919), S.V. Ketkar (1884-1937) and H.H. Risley (1851-1911) and, without being biased towards these well-known authorities, he pointed out the shortcomings of all these scholars in understanding the essential feature of the caste system. But his method of criticism was quite interesting. While criticizing the authorities, Ambedkar did not fail to observe the positive aspects of their contributions. In his words:

> To review these definitions is of great importance for our purpose. It will be noticed that taken individually the definitions of three of the writers include too much or too little: none is complete or correct by itself and all have missed the central point in the mechanism of the caste system. Their mistake lies in trying to define caste as an isolated unit by itself, and not as a group within, and with definite relations to, the system of caste as a whole. Yet, collectively, all of them are complementary to one another, each one emphasizing what has been obscured in the other [Ambedkar (1917): 1979: 7].

Looking at caste as a system in which each *jati* is part of the whole was definitely a step forward in social and cultural anthropology as early as 1917 and Ambedkar was not ready to accept the caste system as a system of 'division of labour' which minimized competition among occupational groups as viewed by N.K. Bose (for him, the caste system is a division among the labouring classes rather than division of labour). A closer reading of this article reveals that, although in the milieu of Boasians at Columbia, Ambedkar used the Morganian social evolutionary methodology to approach the basic principle behind the caste system. He observed that marriage outside one's own immediate kin-group represented through clan exogamy was the fundamental and universal feature of human society and in India the state of 'tribal exogamy' survived even in the stages of civilization whereas in the modern world this is no more the rule. Let me quote from the original:

With the growth of history, however, exogamy has lost its efficacy, and excepting the nearest blood-kins, there is usually no social bar restricting the field of marriage. But regarding the people of India the law of exogamy is a positive injunction even today. Indian society still savours of the clan system, even though there are no clans; and this can be easily seen from the law of matrimony which centres round the principle of exogamy, for it is not that Sapindas (blood-kins) cannot marry, but a marriage even between Sagotras (of the same class) is regarded as a sacrilege [ibid (1917): 1979: 9].

This is the logical foundation based on which Ambedkar advanced his arguments to elucidate the caste system. He cogently argued that since in India exogamy was the stronger rule, endogamy must have been foreign to the country. So then how could the caste system, which had to survive on endogamy, could come into place in India? The way Ambedkar answered this anomaly is the most interesting part of this original paper. Before going into the details let me quote again:

Nothing is, therefore, more important for you to remember than the fact that endogamy is foreign to the people of India. The various Gotras of India are and have been exogamous: so are the other groups with totemic organization. It is no exaggeration to say that with the people of India exogamy is a creed and none dare infringe it, so much so that, in spite of the endogamy of the castes within them, exogamy is strictly observed and that there are more rigorous penalties for violating exogamy than there are for violating endogamy. . . Consequently, in the final analysis, creation of castes, so far as India is concerned, means the superposition of endogamy on exogamy [ibid (1917): 1979: 9].

Next to this analysis Ambedkar went on to explain how some of the social groups in ancient India, which were classes turned into enclosed endogamous groups probably to ensure continuence of the privileges which they accrued out of the ancient class system. According to Ambedkar, since the Brahmin and the Kshatriyas were the most privileged classes, it was these classes that began to enclose themselves to secure their privileges by becoming endogamous. Later, other groups also emulated the higher classes and the system spread over wider regions. So classes in India were forerunner to castes, and castes, according to Ambedkar, were enclosed classes characterized by endogamy. I quote Ambedkar:

We shall be well advised to recall at the outset that the Hindu society, in common with other societies, was composed of classes and the earliest known are (1) the Brahmins or the priestly class; (2) the Kshatriya, or the military class; (3) the Vaishya, or the merchant class; and (4) the Shudra, or the artisan and menial class. Particular attention has to be paid to the fact that this was essentially a class system, in which individuals, when qualified, could change their class, and, therefore, classes did change their personnel. At some time in the history of the Hindus, the priestly class socially detached itself from the rest of the body of people and through a closed-door policy became a caste by itself. The other classes being subject to the law of social division of labour underwent differentiation, some into large, others into very minute, groups. . . . The question we have to answer in this connection is: Why did these sub-divisions or classes, if you please, industrial, religious or otherwise, become self-enclosed or endogamous? My answer is because the Brahmins were so. Endogamy or the closed-door system, was a fashion in the Hindu society, and as it had originated from the Brahmin caste it was whole-heartedly imitated by all the non-Brahmin sub-divisions or classes who, in their turn, became endogamous castes. It is 'the infection of imitation' that caught all these sub-divisions on their onward march of differentiation and has turned them into castes (ibid.: 17-18).

Starting from a fundamental anthropological finding of tribal clan exogamy, Ambedkar had been able to show how caste endogamy was superimposed on the former. Secondly, his exposition of caste as an extreme form of class system as early as 1917 was also exemplary, and this work of Ambedkar was never mentioned or referred to by the world-renowned scholars on caste in India (Guha 2016c & d). I have previously mentioned about G.S. Ghurye. The same kind of omission of the anthropological contributions of B.R. Ambedkar could also be observed in the writings of Nirmal Kumar Bose For example, in his *Economic Weekly* article, 'Class and Caste', published in 1965 (vol. 17, issue 35), Bose admitted that caste can be regarded as a form of class in which the Brahminical classes tried to reserve their privileges in society. Bose did not mention that Ambedkar in his seminal paper in the anthropology seminar had already observed this fact nearly 50 years ago. Interestingly, both Bose and Ambedkar had their own ideas about the origin of caste which were little influenced by Western anthropologists and sociologists. While Ambedkar emphasized more on the endogamy of caste superimposed on tribal exogamy, Bose attempted to view caste as a superior socioeconomic system, which could absorb the less powerful tribal society. Ambedkar's method seemed to be better-knit theoretically than Bose's and the former maintained a kind of academic detachment from his painful personal experiences while presenting the seminar paper on caste at Columbia University. Bose, on the other hand, seemed to be less consistent methodologically and had fallen prey to some simplistic biases which ultimately led him to ignore his own empirical findings (Guha 2018f: 36-40 & 2018d: 105-10). An interesting exception was Gerald Berremen (1930-2013), an American anthropologist, who conducted field work in the 1950s in India and compared caste system and racial discrimination in USA as harmful systems of inequality (Berreman 1960: 120-7). Not unsurprisingly, recent anthropological studies emphasized the similarities between the views of B.R. Ambedkar and G. Berreman although the latter did not quote Ambedkar (*Frontline* 2014).

NOTES

1. The first professional journal of anthropology in India was the *Journal of the Anthropological Society of Bombay* which was founded in 1886. Its first editor was Edward Tyrrell Leith, a British national and professor of law at the Government Law College, Bombay (now Mumbai). This journal continued up to 1973 (Shah 2014: 363).
2. G. Chattopadhyay, 'A Critical Appreciation of Professor K.P. Chattopadhyay's Work on Education', *Life and Times of an Indian Anthropologist: K.P. Chattopadhyay*, ed. G. Chattopadhyay, Calcutta: The Asiatic Society, 2000, pp. 1-7.
3. B.K. Roy Burman, 'Professor K.P. Chattopadhyay: A Scientist with Social Concern', *Life and Times of an Indian Anthropologist: K.P. Chattopadhyay*, ed. G. Chattopadhyay, The Asiatic Society, Calcutta, 2000, pp. 50-1.
4. C. von Haimendorf, Review of *Ancient Indian Culture Contacts and Migrations*, *Bulletin of the School of Oriental and African Studies*, vol. 31, issue 2, Calcutta, 1968, pp. 450-1.
5. N.K. Bose's paper entitled 'Hindu Method of Tribal Absorption' was presented as a lecture in the same Science Congress of 1941 in which T.C. Das delivered the presidential address. Bose's lecture was later published in the journal, *Science and Culture*, and, in course of time, became famous in Indian anthropology whereas Das' lecture dealing with the role of anthropology in solving the burning and practical problems of nation-building went into oblivion among the anthropologists in India.
6. Ambedkar was a student at Columbia from 1913-16. He earned his PhD in Economics from Columbia University in 1927 and D.Sc. in the same subject in 1923 (Krishnamurty 2019: 147-57). His main object of study was economics, but Ambedkar did not limit himself to this discipline. Ambedkar's student records at Columbia show that he took courses in sociology, politics, philosophy, history and even two courses in anthropology that lasted a whole academic year. From 1915 to 1916, Ambedkar attended the course 'General Ethnology: Primitive Man and Physical Environment' and 'General Ethnology: Primitive Religion, Mythology and Social Organisation' (See footnote no. 10 in the article of Cháirez-Garza 2018: 6).

CHAPTER 5

The Future of Nationalist Anthropology in India

I

The future of anthropology in India in the broader context of nation-building cannot be understood without looking into its past. In the previous chapters of this book, I have made an attempt to find out the nationalist trends of anthropological research in India. I have done it through the study of some of the major works of notable anthropologists in India, both in the colonial and post-colonial periods. Now I would again go back to history, this time, a selected portion in the history of anthropology in the post-colonial period. I would particularly look into the question of nation-building and the contributions of the anthropologists in the process because the future of nationalist anthropology depends also on its past. The true nationalist tradition of anthropology in India, or for that matter in any developing country, cannot be understood without looking into the works of the anthropologists who contributed towards the task of nation-building.

II

Virtually no discussion is found on the role of anthropologists in the writings and commentaries of the scholars on the rise and development of nationalism and nationalist thought in India. Even one of the doyens and visionaries of Indian anthropology, Nirmal Kumar Bose, who held important governmental and university positions in post-independent India and was a personal secretary to M.K. Gandhi did not discuss the contributions and role of anthropologists in nation-building in independent India in his two important books entitled *Problems of National Integration* (1967) and *Problems of Indian Nationalism* (1969). In one of his significant articles published in the *Bulletin of the Anthropological Survey of India* in 1962, Bose discussed briefly on some problems and solutions of national integration without mentioning the role and responsibilities of the anthropologists in the task. In the final section of the article, Bose offered the 'Gandhian formula' of decentralization through local governments as the ideal solution towards achieving national integration against provincialism and all kinds of sectarianism (Bose 1962b: 57-61). Only at the end of his life did N.K. Bose emphasize the role of anthropologists in nation-building in his posthumous article.

> An anthropologist does not merely play the part of an observer in a game of chess. He has a greater and deeper commitment, namely, that he has to draw a lesson from what he observes, so that he can utilize his knowledge in the attainment of the egalitarian ideal which our nation has set before itself as its goal. If he also accepts this ideal, then, with his superior analytical apparatus, and the use of comparisons and synthetic thinking, he can suggest many modifications in the ways in which the government or leaders of society are trying to bring about justice where injustice prevails today. And this is where anthropology has a very significant role to play and a heavy responsibility to bear (Bose 1974: iv).

Another doyen of Indian sociology and social anthropology, M.N. Srinivas, in his essay, 'Nation-Building in Independent India' first published in 1976, expressed his scepticism regarding the contributions of social scientists in understanding the 'significance as well as complexity of political and social stability for a vast and developing country such as India' (Srinivas 2009: 390). Srinivas, however, in his article entitled 'The Development of Sociology and Social Anthropology' jointly written with M.N. Panini and first published in *Sociological Bulletin* in 1973, observed 'a sharp increase in the popularity of the two disciplines' in the post-independence period and they also noted the effect of the creation of the National Planning Commission on the development of the social sciences (Srinivas & Panini 1973: 197).[1] But in the same article we do not find any reference to the anthropological works done on the problems of the resettlement of refugees, famine of Bengal and displacement caused by industries and dams, which posed great challenges to nation-building in its early period.[2] In L.P. Vidyarthi's two-volume *Rise of Anthropology in India* (1978), we also do not find any particular reference to the aforementioned topics as part of the nation-building process. The renowned social anthropologist Gopala Sarana, in his article, 'The Study of the Nation-Building Process', published in 1974 on the occasion of the 50th anniversary of the University of Calcutta, dealt with some theoretical issues and ended his discussion by making some futuristic hopes on the usefulness of anthropology towards nation-building in India (Sarana 1974: 30-41). In more recent periods the non-anthropologists (economists, historians and political scientists), who debated the problems of nationalism and nation-building in India, missed the contributions of anthropologists made towards nation-building during the early years after independence. All the discussions of these scholars centred round theoretical issues on the definition and ideas of nationalism, civil society, communalism versus nationalism, Hindu nationalism, globalization and nationalism, nationalism as an ideology, Rabindranath Tagore, Bankimchandra Chattopadhyay, Aurobindo Ghose, and B.R. Ambedkar's ideas on nationalism but there was virtually nothing on the practice of nation-building in post-independence India, let alone the anthropological contributions on the subject (see for example, Pandey 1987; Chatterjee 1997; Gaikwad 1998; Nandy 2006; Sarkar 2006; Sen 2008; Bhattacharya 2016; Srivastava 2012; Palit & Sengupta 2016; Dubey 2017). Under this broader intellectual context, I will concentrate on the following question. Were there anthropological studies done to address some of the vital problems faced by the policy makers of independent India in the early years after independence of the country? In particular, did the anthropologists study (a) famine, (b) partition and resettlement of refugees, and (c) socio-economic impact of mega-industrialisation and dam building? Undoubtedly, these three were among the major challenges which not only confronted post-independent India in its early years but continued to persist for a long period of time.

III

One of the important areas in which anthropologists have consistently contributed is the bio-cultural study of ethnic minorities, variously labelled as tribes, aboriginals, autochthones, indigenous communities and adivasis. A related area of focus of the anthropologists was the marginalised condition of these communities and also about how to ameliorate the condition of these communities and integrate them in the mainstream of the Indian nation in the post-independence period of the country. It is important to note that the contributions of the anthropologists towards nation-building in the post-independence period of India were hardly considered to be important by the planners and policymakers partly because of the nature of the discipline and in part owing to the avoidance of the anthropologists in situating their micro-level studies in the wider or macro context of the nation.[3] Therefore, the detailed empirical studies on particular tribes, castes and villages made little sense to the makers of the Five-Year Plans of the country. Anthropologists were definitely regarded as experts on tribal policy at the national level but compared to economists their presence in nation-building or national planning was marginal. Even when the value of anthropological methodology of conducting in-depth field based studies were understood, it was practically not feasible for the government to engage a sufficient number of trained anthropologists to make plans for displaced persons affected by famine, partition, industrialization or dam-building in the country by properly assessing the micro-level social impacts of these mega-events as occurring in post-colonial India.[4] Anthropologists, themselves too, were largely satisfied with their position as experts on tribes, pursuing only their professional and technical research on tribal welfare and development across the length and breadth of the country long after independence (see for example, Vidyarthi 1972: 80-93; Sahay 1998: 73-81). As a consequence, the Indian anthropologists remained on the margins of nation-building, pursuing their micro-level studies on tribes and some caste populations, sometimes almost in the fashion of their colonial masters either from the Anthropological Survey of India or from various university departments. Applied anthropology for the anthropologists in India became planning and development for tribals (Sachahidananda 1973: 1-16). In a calendrical account on 'Some Landmarks of Indian Anthropology' published in 1986 in *Human Science*, the official journal of the Anthropological Survey of India, only three events were recorded under 1951 which have a direct bearing on national level planning, viz., (i) application of anthropological research findings in the implementation of community development project, (ii) application of anthropology in the formation of panchayati raj system, and (iii) creation of separate departments and agencies in the governments for the study of Scheduled Caste, Scheduled Tribe and Other Backward Communities (Bose 1986: 74-6). In 1986, a national seminar, titled 'Anthropology in the Service of Nation', was organized jointly by the Indian Anthropological Association and Anthropological Survey of India and 22 papers presented in the seminar were published in the form of a book under the title *Anthropology Development and Nation Building* in 1987 edited by A.K. Kalla and K.S. Singh. In the preface, the editors, after explaining the importance of anthropology in planning and development, mentioned their objective in the following manner:

> . . . the Indian Anthropological Association and the Anthropological Survey of India decided to explore together the latest trends of research which have significant implications for the urgent task of nation-building in all its aspects (Kalla & Singh 1987: v).

The papers in the book covered health, nutrition, population structure, problems of women, development of backward areas, displacement and resettlement, environment, ethnicity, communal harmony and national integration. None of the chapters in the volume made any attempt to search and assess the pioneering works done by the Indian anthropologists which were part of the nation-building process in its early phase.[5] There was no effort by the anthropologists who contributed in the aforementioned book to look into the past records as regards the pioneering contributions in the discipline towards the study of the three major challenges (famine, partition, industrialization and dam-building) encountered by the policy makers of the then new nation.[6] Similar kind of omission was also found in a review article published after more than two decades (the Kalla and Singh book) written by B. Chaudhuri (Chaudhuri 2015: 1-14).

The foregoing narrative, however, should not lead one to conclude that Indian anthropologists did not think about situating their subject and findings in the context of nation-building. In the next section, I will first recount two early anthropological discourses on nation building in India.

IV

As early as 1941, Tarak Chandra Das in his presidential address in the anthropology section of the Indian Science Congress, dealt with the application of the subject in almost all the important sectors of a modern nation, viz., trade, industry, agriculture, legislation, education, social service and administration. The lecture was a 28-page full-length paper entitled, 'Cultural Anthropology in the Service of the Individual and the Nation'. In this lecture, Das' major objective was to convince his readers about the immense potential of social-cultural anthropology as applied science for the overall development of the Indian population (Das 1941: 1-29). The message concerning the role of anthropologists in nation building delivered by T.C. Das was carried forward by S.S. Sarkar, another doyen of Indian anthropology, again from the University of Calcutta, and he was a biological anthropologist.

His presidential address in the anthropology section was entitled, 'The Place of Human Biology in Anthropology and its Utility in the Service of the Nation'. It was delivered in 1951 in the Indian Science Congress and later published in *Man in India*. In the lecture, Sarkar mentioned Das' strong recommendation towards turning the Widow Remarriage Act from a 'permissive' to a 'coercive' one in the interest of 'national welfare'. Throughout his lecture, Sarkar cited example after example from various studies conducted by physical anthropologists and human biologists all over the world which have had enormous policy implications towards nation building in India (Sarkar 1951: 1-22).

In a much later period, the human biology approach of S.S. Sarkar was carried forward by his student Amitabha Basu at the Indian Statistical Institute Kolkata during the 1960s and 70s. In 1987, Basu wrote a comprehensive historical article, entitled 'Human Biology in India: Its Possible Role in a Third World Society under Rapid Transformation', in a prestigious international journal named *Collegium Anthropologicum* by following Sarkar's basic guideline of building a healthy nation through the making of individuals healthy in body and mind. In this unique article, Basu narrated how colonial 'Physical Anthropology' (represented by H.H. Risley and his classification of the Indian population into 'Races') gradually transformed into a much wider 'Human Biology', which devoted itself to the task of building a healthy nation. According to Basu, the role of human biology towards the service of the independent nation is not simply like that of a biological science.

The most important and special role of human biology, following from the tradition of its precursor discipline physical anthropology, is to consider at the micro-level, and on the basis of detailed, intensive and firsthand information collection, a multitude of human biological traits (not merely disease traits) and the totality of their environmental and genetic backgrounds, in order to detect and measure the intricacies of their interrelations and interactions. This role we presume is most advantageous in view of the immense variability of the human physiological functioning and social behaviour in predicting the course of biological, social and biosocial changes in Third World societies and directing the course, if even to a limited extent, in a meaningful direction (Basu 1987: 248).[7]

It is important here to note that this 'biosocial' dimension of human existence is the unique thrust area of anthropology, which distinguished the discipline from sociology and this integrated approach was also discernible in the pioneering works of T.C. Das, B.S. Guha, Surajit Sinha and Irawati Karve, all of which I have described in the following sections.

V

Under this general scenario of anthropological discourse around nation-building, a specific focus could also be discerned in the works of the anthropologists in India. This focus was centered towards the (i) displacement, and resettlement of populations caused by famine, (ii) partition of the country on religious grounds during independence, and (iii) industrialization and dam-building by the state in the initial years of mega-planning under the First and Second Five Years Plans. All the three events, i.e. famine, partition and mega-development efforts (industrialization and dam-building) were inseparable from nation-building, and policymakers needed anthropological advocacy and insight to deal with the problems arising out of displacement caused by partition and mega-development efforts. Definitely, the anthropological interventions in these mega events of nation-building were miniscule in proportion to the nationwide magnitude of those episodes. But in terms of the intensive nature and quality of the micro-level findings, the anthropological studies on refugee resettlement and rehabilitation and development caused displaced persons offer a new area around the discourse on nationalism, so far untouched by historians, economists and political scientists. How the suggestions and recommendations of the anthropologists were adopted by the policymakers in these cases is a different issue, which is not within the ambit of this research.

VI

It would not be out of place to discuss here about the role of the Anthropological Survey of India, which is the largest governmental organisation of anthropology in the country, as regards development caused displacement and rehabilitation of project-affected families. In India, there is no governmental or non-governmental source of data on the nature, extent and degree of food shortage and its consequent effects on the biology on the different population groups caused by land acquisition for any period. The government and the anthropologists have also not collected or published any data on how people in different places have also been adapting, both biologically and culturally, under stress. The stress that is caused by the acquisition of their land, a vital life support system, of the majority of tribal populations in the country. The largest and the only governmental organization, the Anthropological Survey of India, collected huge amount of data on the tribes and castes of India in the fashion of the anthropologists of the Empire. Not a single piece of information was collected on any tribe or caste of India as regards the bio-cultural impacts of land acquisition which took place all around the country regarding the endangerment of food security and its after-effects by the application of the land acquisition law. It was only in November 2010 that the Anthropological Survey of India prepared a module for conducting Socio-economic Impact Assessment (SEIA) in the country. The document is a 40-page text which dealt in detail about the social impact assessment, mainly as a 'timely academic and research-oriented exercise needed by the country' (Anthropological Survey of India 2010). As of today, no data have yet been published by the Anthropological Survey of India on the various bio-cultural impacts of land acquisition on the tribal and other populations of India. The SEIA by the largest governmental organization remained a purely academic pursuit. To be frank, the Indian anthropologists, while following the trail of the British census commissioners, have produced a mass of anthropological information which could not be of any applied or practical value for dealing with the vital governmental decision of going with or without SEIA and the consent clauses of the post-independence land acquisition law. A glaring example of post-colonial governmental anthropology is the People of India Project undertaken by the Anthropological Survey of India in 1985. The results of this project were published throughout the 1990s. A total of 600 anthropologists participated in the study of 4,693 'communities' conducted in all the states and union territories in India. The reports contained data on the biological and cultural aspects of the populations of India. But there is virtually no information on the impact of various development projects for which land was being acquired from under the feet of these people. The reports were no more than traditional ethnographic accounts of the tribes and castes of India almost in the fashion done by H.H. Risely about a hundred years ago (Jenkins 2003: 1143: 70). By contrast, the earlier surveys of the British census commissioners were of great use for the colonial administration in running the Empire in India (Guha 2017b: 23-5). A noted anthropologist, D.K. Bhattacharya, who was a prehistorian, rather bravely observed the 'silence' of the anthropologists in India over the sanction of the Sardar Sarovar dam by the government, in his scathing editorial in *Indian Anthropologist*. I quote Bhattacharya:

> The recent sanction of the Government of India for the implementation of the mammoth dams to be built across the Narmada, has been a calculated strategy adopted by the developmentalists and not objected to, in fact, silently approved of by the anthropologists wedded to what I have called the 'Planning Commissionist' way of thinking. Here we are bartering away thousands of acres of forest teeming with a fantastically rich faunal and floral wealth and at least three tribal groups constituting thousands. Depriving so many of so much for the sake of a paltry couple of thousands of megawatts of electricity. Even this electricity is certainly going to be used to produce consumerist goods! Not a single anthropologist has either been consulted or has raised his voice against this form of development (Bhattacharya 1991: 2).

In the aforementioned editorial, Bhattacharya, however, did not mention the remarkable earlier works done by the anthropologists on development-caused displacement during the early years after independence of the country, which I will take up in the next section of this chapter.

VII

For the purpose of this study towards the exploration of anthropological discourses around resettlement and rehabilitation of famine-affected destitutes, refugees of partition and development project-affected populations, I have selected five pioneering studies conducted by eminent anthropologists who made important contributions in solving the aforementioned problems encountered by independent India. All the studies were published after the independence of the country and, except the study on Bengal famine by Tarak Chandra Das, the rest of the studies were conducted within the span of the first four Five Year Plans of India during 1951-74. I enumerate the studies below in their chronological order.

1. *Bengal Famine (1943): As Revealed in a Survey of the Destitutes of Calcutta* (1949) by Tarak Chandra Das, the University of Calcutta.
2. *Resettlement of East Pakistan Refugees in Andaman Islands: Report on Survey of Further Possibilities of Resettlement* (1955) by Surajit Chandra Sinha, Government of West Bengal.
3. *Studies in Social Tensions Among the Refugees From Eastern Pakistan* (1959) by B.S. Guha, department of anthropology, Government of India.
4. *Social Processes in the Industrialization of Rourkela (With Reference to Displacement and Rehabilitation of Tribal and Other Backward People)* (1961) by B.K. Roy Burman, Office of the Registrar General, India.
5. *A Survey of the People Displaced Through the Koyna Dam* (1969), by Irawati Karve and Jai Nimbkar, Deccan College, Pune.

The first common feature of these anthropological studies was that, except the study done by T.C. Das on Bengal famine, all of them were commissioned and sponsored either by the central or the state government of independent India which engaged anthropologists on matters related to displacement and resettlement.[8] Das' study was funded partly in its later stage by the University of Calcutta. The second feature of these studies was that they were not specifically directed to any particular ethnic minority or community, as had been done by the anthropologists following the colonial tradition, but on the populations affected by partition and development processes. The third common denominator of these studies was their focus on the collection of both social and biological data (read demographic) and the creation of a solid empirical database. In all these studies, the main objective of the authors was to collect, organize and analyze quantitative and qualitative data on the problem, which they wanted to investigate. Fourth, the analyses of the data were also done not to test or generate any theory or hypothesis as regards the human populations, societies and cultures involved in the processes but to collect concrete factual materials on the ground realities of displacement of human populations in the newly independent nation. Fifth, in all the studies, we find that the anthropologists innovatively employed their traditional methods (participant observation, genealogy, case study, etc.) to large populations. Finally, these studies were done not only for seeking pure knowledge but also to generate policies around the major challenges encountered by the planners of the newly independent country in the post-colonial period. In short, these studies can be viewed as sincere attempts by the anthropologists towards the making of a new nation and that still remains outside the mainstream debates and discussion around nation-building by the social scientists and even among the anthropologists themselves.

VIII

T.C. Das (1898-1964) was one of the founder teachers of the oldest anthropology department of India at Calcutta University and he was famous for his ethnographic fieldwork. He conducted fieldwork to assess the impact of industrialization in Birlapur in West Bengal, and wrote thought-provoking articles containing anthropological and sociological analyses on the Bengal dowry restriction bill of 1940 and the Hindu code bill in the years 1940 and 1944 along with articles on the practical suggestions for the improvement of museums in India (Ray 1974: 56-60). Das' book on the famine of Bengal, which took place in 1943, was a unique and rare first-hand study done by an anthropologist on the victims of one of the greatest tragedies of our country under the colonial rule. An earlier version of the book was discussed in the then British parliament and some of the recommendations advanced by Das were adopted by the Famine Inquiry Commission in 1944 formed by the colonial government for the prevention of future famines in India (Das 1949: iii-iv). The first Prime Minister of independent India, Jawaharlal Nehru, in his book *The Discovery of India*, mentioned the anthropological survey conducted by Das on the famine-affected population of Bengal and expressed his confidence on the results of the survey in contrast to the one carried out by the government (Nehru 1946: 495-6). Ironically enough, the Nobel laureate economist Amartya Sen while referring to Das' original study several times in his famous book *Poverty and Famines*, did not mention the explanatory and policy dimensions of this brilliant work (Sen 1999; see Guha, 2019 for an elaborate discussion on this subject). It is relevant here to mention that Ramkrishna Mukherjee, jointly with P.C. Mahalanobis, conducted their well-known statistical survey on the after effects of Bengal famine which was published in 1946 (Mahalanobis, Mukherjea and Ghosh 1946: 337-400) and was mentioned by T.C. Das in the preface of his book on the famine (Das 1949: iii).

The subtitle of the book *Bengal Famine* is phrased in the following words: 'As Revealed in a Survey of the Destitutes in Calcutta'. It is true that the book is the result of a survey undertaken by a team of anthropologists during 1943-4 in Calcutta city and also in the villages of the 10 districts of undivided Bengal. The idea of conducting a survey with a team of trained anthropologists was first conceived by T.C. Das in July-August of 1943 when hundreds of hungry destitutes entered the city of Calcutta in search of food. Das proposed the survey to his colleagues and prepared a detailed questionnaire and a team was formed with 11 trained anthropologists, which included the teachers and research students of the department of anthropology of the Calcutta University. The data thus collected were analyzed, a preliminary report written and a major part of the report was submitted to the Famine Inquiry Commission in 1944 in the form of a memorandum. The report was later compiled in the form of a book by T.C. Das in July 1948 and published in 1949 by the Calcutta University. This anthropological survey was conducted with full methodological rigour and the team had no national or international funding agency behind them; no political agenda was lying before them. The Calcutta University sanctioned a sum of Rs. 500 only to extend the survey in the rural areas of the 10 districts of erstwhile undivided Bengal. In fact, the two chapters on methodology, which are the best portions of the book, revealed its strength. Chapter XI of the book, entitled 'Causes of the Famine of 1943', is another treasure-house. It places the book, *Bengal Famine*, far above the category of a run-of-the-mill 'sample survey'. The first prime miniser of India, Jawaharlal Nehru in his book, *The Discovery of India* (1946), mentioned about the survey in *Bengal Famine* before the publication of the book by T.C. Das and expressed his confidence in the results of the survey in contrast to the one carried out by the government. In the words of Nehru:

> The department of anthropology of the Calcutta University carried out an extensive scientific survey of the sample groups in the famine areas. They arrived at the figure of about 3,400,000 total deaths by famine in Bengal. . . . Official figures of the Bengal government based largely on unreliable reports from village patwaris or headmen gave a much lower figure (Nehru 1946: 495-6).

The 10 chapters of *Bengal Famine* dealt elaborately with the demographic, economic and socio-cultural aspects of one of the greatest calamities of Bengal in the colonial period but the most important section is the final chapter of the book in which Das dealt with the rehabilitative and preventive measures to tackle the famine. Before moving to the section, let me add that Das had thoroughly studied the demographic scenario of famine in terms of (i) age-sex distribution, (ii) marital condition, and the (iii) death rate among the famine-affected destitutes (Das 1949: 33-51 & 90-4). The section, entitled 'How To Combat Famine', is divided into two subsections, viz., (A) long range measures, and (B) immediate measures. Let us first discuss about the 'immediate measures' suggested by Das. Within a short space, Das was able to outline the short-term strategies for bringing relief to the famine-affected population which, according to him, should first involve rapid surveys to identify the specific needs of the people according to region, occupation and the nature of devastation. In order to illustrate his ideas, he dealt with the petty cultivators, fishermen and the potters since the first represented the largest group in the economic life of Bengal, the second was the largest rural industry and the third was the most important artisan group in rural Bengal (Das 1949: 127).

Under the long-range measures, Das' recommendations followed his analysis of causes of the famine. He strongly recommended that in order to avoid future food shortages, heavy pressure on land in Bengal must be relieved and this could be done in adopting two interrelated approaches, viz., (i) improvement of agriculture, and (ii) development of industries. For Das, improvement in agriculture did not mean a mere increase in food production with better technology but to change the relations of production through co-operative farming.[9] The co-operative farming according to Das should have been linked up with the village industries which were to be built up for creating employment for the rural population. In the final section of *Bengal Famine*, he worked out a plan in detail about the formation of such co-operatives and their tasks. I quote from the original:

The innumerable fragments of cultivable land possessed by the inhabitants of a village or of any other similar territorial unit are to be pooled together into one gigantic farm.... All the villagers are to be members of this co-operative organization. The capital of the organisation is to be divided into a number of shares. The owners of the plots of land will get shares of the organization according to the market value of the plots of land taken from them. The remaining part of the capital is to be realized from the inhabitants of the village by selling the shares. The maximum number of shares which an individual will be entitled to purchase is to be fixed according to the principle of co-operative organizations. The co-operative organization will take up the management of the farm and factory. As a general rule, the shareholders are to be employed in all the different types of work of the farm and of the factory, as far as possible (Das 1949: 124-5).

The improvement of agriculture in Bengal through the formation of co-operatives seemed to be the best solution for Das in the context of small, scattered and fragmented landholdings. But at the same time he was also aware of the fact that pooling together of the small-sized farms into a large one would lead to the unemployment of quite a good number of persons engaged in agriculture. To tackle with this problem Das suggested that agriculture-based industries should be established to absorb the labour force no more required for agriculture. In the words of Das:

Rice husking and hessian making may be profitably started in rice and jute producing centers, respectively, for employment of labour not required for farming. Fruit canning may be organized where fruit gardens are planted. Cheroots may be made where tobacco is cultivated. Silk and lac may also be utilized in the same manner in the area where they are produced. In this way there should be co-ordination and co-operation between the farm and the factory—one is to utilize the products of the other as far as possible (ibid. 1949: 125).

It was obvious that the implementation of this kind of programme leading to radical changes in policy on the part of the government could not be done simply by the good intentions and neatly chalked out plans alone. The programme also needed a thorough knowledge about the villages and this, according to Das, could only be acquired through 'village studies'. In the concluding part of the section entitled 'How To Combat Famine', Das lamented by saying:

> To implement this policy an intimate knowledge of the villages and villagers is absolutely necessary. For this purpose, a socio-economic survey should be organized with a band of scientifically trained men. We have got archaeological survey, zoological survey, geological survey, botanical survey but no survey to understand man and his social, economic and psychological needs. This is an anomalous position. . . . The result is that whenever the government is confronted with a national catastrophe like the present famine it has no knowledge to guide its activities—no trained men to depend upon (ibid 1949: 129-30).

Bengal Famine, therefore, is a unique example of teamwork under the leadership of T.C. Das by a dedicated group of university based anthropologists who were driven more by a kind of social and moral commitment towards nation and its people than by a pure academic quest (Guha 2019b: 493-506). We may note here that the Anthropological Survey of India was established in 1946 but it could not draw the attention of Das as regards the Bengal famine and its devastating socio-economic and biological impact. Suffice it to say that the governmental organization could not carry out any survey on Bengal famine at that time or even later.

IX

I will now take up the study undertaken by Surajit Sinha (1926-2002), who had then just received his M.Sc. degree in anthropology from the University of Calcutta.[10] Sinha went on to become a famous anthropologist in post-independent India who was later director of the Anthropological Survey of India and well-known for his contribution to the study of tribal and caste societies of India in the context of the greater Indian civilization. Sinha's painstaking and intensive study on the resettlement of the Bengali refugee population in Andaman just after the partition of the country still remains an unnoticed work in the history of Indian anthropology. An interesting example is the special issue of the *Journal of the Indian Anthropological Society* published in 2003, in memory of Surajit Chandra Sinha, containing 26 articles by eminent scholars including the author of this book. We do not find any article on the Andaman study of Sinha except passing remarks of admiration of this work of Sinha (see for example, Chakrabarti 2003: 103-6; Misra 2003: 139-57; Ghosh 2003: 111-15; Sarkar 2003: 167-72). S.B. Chakrabarti in an earlier article mentioned that Sinha's report on the resettlement of Bengali refugees in Andaman was 'excellent' but went 'unnoticed' although in the same article under the 'chronology of events' in the life of Sinha he omitted the work of Sinha on Andaman (Chakrabarti 2002: 189-95). This study can be viewed as one of the pioneering anthropological works on nation-building since it dealt scientifically with the burning problem of refugee resettlement which was plaguing the planners and administrators of the new nation. Sinha was appointed by the refugee rehabilitation department of the government of West Bengal in 1951 as an anthropologist. His task was to visit the Andaman Islands and report to the state and central governments on the possibilities of further resettlement of families displaced from then East Pakistan by studying the local situation as regards the relationship between the refugees and the host populations of Andaman Islands. In the very beginning of the report, Sinha categorically stated his objective in the following manner:

> A student of cultural anthropology has a distinctive point of view in approaching socio-economic problems. Any social situation is assessed by him in terms of how far it satisfies the total range of human needs in the communities under observation. His attention is not restricted to economic plans only; the problems of social relationship and other cultural factors are given simultaneous consideration. So, the problem of relationship between the refugees and original inhabitants was not studied as an isolated item (Sinha 1955: 1).

After outlining his anthropological position, Sinha stated the specific objectives of the study in concrete terms, which were (i) intensive socio-economic survey of the resettled refugees, (ii) comparison of the degree of adaptation of the refugees and the earlier settlers, (iii) socio-economic interrelation between refugees and earlier settlers, and (iv) identification of suitable geographical areas in the Andaman Islands for further rehabilitation of refugees. Most interestingly, Sinha's intensive socio-economic and demographic survey not only included collection of quantitative data but also the participatory observation of the whole round of daily activities of the resettled refugees. He even took part in their 'gossips to note the psychological trends, on which direct questionnaire method or statistical enquiry did not seem profitable' (ibid). The demographic and socio-economic survey conducted by Sinha is one of the finest examples of an anthropological study on resettlement and rehabilitation of displaced families in India. For example, he has not only collected economic information but also quantitative data on the age-sex distribution, marital condition and birth rate of the refugee population (Sinha 1955: 5-7). His study contained detailed factual descriptions of the historical background, geographical environment, socio-demographic features, settlement pattern, economic and social life of the resettled refugee population in Andaman. The description vividly revealed the ground realities of resettlement around the differential adaptation of the refugee groups and Sinha was not hesitant to record the failures of the government in providing land for the resettlers. With the help of quantitative data presented in the form of a table Sinha stated:

> The chart amply shows that not only the promised quota of land has not been fulfilled in most cases, but there also exists a large amount of disparity in distribution of land among the different settlers. This has hindered the attachment of the refugees to the local soil. They are still in the hope that they may be given their full quota of land somewhere else. The refugees allege that their lands have not been measured to their satisfaction (ibid. 1955: 14).

Along with governmental failures, Sinha also noted the limitations of the refugees in adapting to the new environment. On page 24 of the report, we find:

On the whole the refugees are even today dissipating some amount of their energies in grumbling and praying for more grants than adequately exploiting their allotted quota of land. Though the cultivator families are doing fairly well in tilling the plain lands, their record in clearing jungles for expanding the cultivable land has been poor. They have moved very little in exploiting the forest or sea (ibid. 1955: 24).

However, immediately after making the above statement Sinha provided some positive examples of traditional higher caste (Brahmin and Kayastha) families among the refugees who had started ploughing land and also some resettlers whom he found to have been working hard clearing the jungles. Quite importantly, Sinha's fieldwork was not limited to the Bengali refugees. He devoted adequate time to understand the complex situation of adaptation of the earlier settlers in Andaman, which included the descendents of Indian convict parents, the Mapillas, the Bhantus, the Burmans, the Karens and the Madrasi refugees from then Rangoon. In a section entitled 'Local Adaptation of the East Pakistan Refugees Compared with the Earlier Settlers', Sinha carefully depicted how the different groups adapted to the Andaman situation under a variety of historical and socio-economic factors and how these earlier settlers maintained a peaceful relationship with the later Bengali refugees who were last of the series of re-settlers on the islands. Finally, Sinha made a comprehensive assessment on the whole situation of refugee resettlement in Andaman and provided point-by-point practical recommendations on further possibilities of a more planned refugee resettlement on different parts of Andaman Islands with transparency and consultation with the refugees themselves.

X

Biraja Sankar Guha (1894-1961) was the founder of the Anthropological Survey of India and known to students of anthropology as a physical anthropologist who made a classification of the Indian population on the basis of their physical features

(Ray 1956: 38-44). Very few know that he was the first to undertake a thorough field survey on social tensions among refugees of then East Pakistan for advising the government about how to understand their problems and improve their living conditions (Guha 1959).

The book by B.S. Guha on social tension was based on intensive fieldwork done by an interdisciplinary team of researchers. The book is basically a solid factual report and analysis of socio-economic, cultural and psychological data collected by a team of trained anthropologists and psychologists on the refugees who came from then East Pakistan to West Bengal under the overall supervision of B.S. Guha.[11] In his general introduction, Guha first justified his selection of two sample areas of refugee resettlement colonies which he finalized in consultation with Gardener Murphy who was selected by the UNESCO as consultant to the Government of India in the project to understand the underlying causes of social tension in India. After this, and I have already pointed out that Guha placed the survey in the wider political scenario of the country and mentioned in unequivocal terms the evil effects of the 'divide and rule' policy of the British government as well as the sectarian approach of the Muslim League government of the then Bengal, which paved the way towards 'engineered' communal riots that led to large scale displacement of the Hindus from East Pakistan (Guha 1959: viii). While researching the reasons behind the evacuation of the Hindus, Guha based his arguments not on any sociological theory but on the empirical findings of his multidisciplinary team of fieldworkers. Therefore, according to him:

> The loss of prestige and social status which the Hindu community previously enjoyed, and the realization of the futility of regaining it now or in the near future was a far more potent factor in creating the feeling of frustration than the loss in the economic sphere (ibid. 1959: viii).

In the subsequent pages of the introduction, Guha went on to analyze the data on the 'areas of tension' among the Hindu refugees which were collected by his research team members through the use of social anthropological and psychological methods. Guha here made an excellent sociological analysis by putting the areas of social tension in a hierarchical and dynamic form. For Guha, his data led him to show how the areas of tension played their respective roles and how the affected members of the community shifted their grievance and aggression from one area of tension to another. Like a true social anthropologist, Guha also ventured into the variation in the social tension at the level of age, sex and sociopolitical situation. Another interesting explanation of B.S. Guha was on the changing authority structure of the traditional Hindu joint family and the worsening of the intra-family relationships among the refugees but here too, he made a comparative interpretation of the two refugee settlements which were selected by him for the study. In one place, where people depended on governmental aid and assistance, the traditional authority structure of the family was found to be stronger than in the refugee colony where the uprooted people had to struggle harder to get themselves resettled (ibid. 1959: xi-xii). By and large what was most interesting to observe was Guha's technique of explaining such a complex phenomenon like social tension. All through, he, like a seasoned sociologist or social anthropologist, attacked the problem from a relational and dynamic angle without falling into the trap of a static view of society (Guha 2018b: 1-12). Finally, and what was really several steps ahead of his time, Guha recommended a participatory and nationalist model for the resettlement of the refugees. For him, the social tension between the refugees and the government mainly arose owing to the fact that they were treated as 'outsiders' from the governmental side. The refugees should be given the responsibility of managing their own resettlement camps so that they could regain their self-respect. I will end by quoting the last line from the Guha's introduction in the book on social tensions:

> Once their displaced energies are canalized into well-directed productive sources, there is every reason to hope, that instead of a burden

and a clog, the refugees will turn out to be useful participants in the march of progress of this country (ibid. 1959: xiii).

In this connection, it is relevant here to mention an empirical study done by Kanti Pakrasi, an anthropologist of the Indian Statistical Institute, on the social behaviour of the refugees from the then East Pakistan. Pakrasi did his intensive anthropological field survey among 11,880 refugee families in 1947-8 as part of a larger socioeconomic survey undertaken by the Indian Statistical Institute and his articles were published in important Indian journals like *Sociological Bulletin*, *Man in India* and *Indian Journal of Social Research* (Pakrasi 1965: 13-20; 1966: 143-52 & 1967: 200-10). The findings of Pakrasi were no less interesting than that of B.S. Guha. For example, Pakrasi found that the numerically dominant group of the refugee families belonged to various non-agricultural occupations and, secondly, irrespective of occupation, a significant number of these refugee households maintained joint family structure (Pakrasi 1965: 209). The most interesting anthropological finding of Pakrasi was the 'persistence of the cultural form of the Hindu way of family living' which was 'most likely the essential determinant in preserving ultimately the kinship solidarity in as high as 92 per cent of all the total family units surveyed' (ibid. 209-10).

XI

B.K. Roy Burman (1922-2012) studied anthropology at the University of Calcutta, and, like Surajit Sinha, he was also trained by T.C. Das (Roy Burman 1978: 107-116). Later, he was advisor to many governmental committees for the welfare of the Scheduled Tribes in India.

In 1960, B.K. Roy Burman, as assistant commissioner for Scheduled Castes and Scheduled Tribes, Government of India, got interested in undertaking an anthropological study on the problems of the tribal and other populations who were displaced by the establishment of the huge public sector steel factory at Rourkela in Orissa. Upon his suggestion, the study of the 'Social Processes in the Industrialization of Rourkela' was taken up as a project for being investigated by the Census Organization. The study was carried out by a team under the leadership of Roy Burman and the results were published by him under the monograph Series of the *Census of India, 1961.* It is not only the first social impact assessment research on industrialization in India but one of the pioneering studies on development caused forced displacement and resettlement at the global level (Cernea 1995: 96). The gigantic plant at Rourkela was the first public sector integrated steel plant with an annual installed capacity to produce one million tonnes of steel. In the introduction of his monograph, Roy Burman emphatically stated the purpose of the study:

> The setting up of the plant was a landmark in the strides of the nation towards progress and prosperity. But it also meant displacement of a large number of persons—mostly tribals—who inhabited the region before the plant was set up. Many of the displaced persons could ultimately re-establish their homes; many could even improve their lots, but at the same time many homes were disrupted; many individuals found themselves hurled at the bottom of an abyss. It is this human aspect of the growth of the giant enterprise at Rourkela that the present study proposes to cover (Roy Burman 1961: 1).

In the rest of this exemplary monograph, which contained 163 pages, we find detailed description of the ecological setting of the steel project and a thorough analysis of the demographic, economic, social, political and religious aspects of about 15,200 displaced population in 30 villages. Along with these, Roy Burman meticulously discussed the extent of rehabilitation and the patterns of new life with new hopes and frustrations that emerged out of this mega development project undertaken in the early years of independence of the country.

The book contains a plethora of quantitative and qualitative data (presented in 121 tables) not only on the spatial and economic consequences of forced displacement but also on its demographic, social, political, psychological and cultural fallouts. For example, we find in the book a number of tables on the views and attitudes of the rehabilitated persons on their job satisfaction (tables 109-11), as well as their frequency of spending time with job mates beyond office hours (tables 114-16). One of the most valuable aspects of this study is Roy Burman's incisive sociological analysis of the social and political processes before and after displacement and that has raised the research far beyond a run-of-the-mill technical social impact assessment report. With massive data and a humanistic approach towards mega industrialisation, Roy Burman, through his penetrating sociological analysis, discovered the strength of the moral order of the society at the village level, which ultimately resulted a greater bargaining power to the displaced families in terms of higher compensation rates, land-for-land and employment in the industry (ibid. 1961: 159-63). The only comparable anthropological study on development-caused displacement in the same period was done by Pranab Kumar Dasgupta of the Anthropological Survey of India. He started field work in the industrial town of Chittaranjan, West Bengal, during 1962-4 to look into the impact of Chittaranjan Locomotive Works (a public sector industry) on the Santal community living in the neighbouring villages of the industry (*Newsletter* 1973). Dasgupta published his detailed findings in 1964 and 1965 which revealed the importance of carrying out anthropological studies on the establishment of huge industrial centres as envisioned in the First and Second Five Year Plans in India (Dasgupta 1964: 85-106; 1965: 76-82).

XII

Irawati Karve (1905-70) was one of the pioneering anthropologists in India who taught anthropology at Deccan College and founded the department of anthropology at the University of Pune (Ray: 162-74). Karve contributed profusely in both physical and social anthropology. Her lesser-known book with Jai Nimbkar, entitled *A Survey of the People Displaced Through the Koyna Dam* (1969), was the first-of-its-kind on displacement caused by a big dam in India. Nandini Sundar perceptively observed that this research is a model for studies on dam-displaced people which received fresh attention in the 1980s and 1990s (Sundar 2010: 405). The study was undertaken by Karve on behalf of the research committee of the Planning Commission of India and was published by Deccan College, Pune. The Koyna dam was the first big project in Maharashtra in which 100 villages were affected involving 30,000 people. A total of 30,000 acres of land under cultivation was submerged and another 32,000 land was acquired, which could no longer be cultivated. But this dam was also the first big project in which the government assumed the responsibility of offering substitute land and housing plots to the displaced families apart from the payment of monetary compensation. With this background, Karve and Nimbkar made a detailed micro-level anthropological investigation to assess the success and failure of governmental rehabilitation and the nature of adaptation of the displaced population. This impact assessment research showed how anthropological methodology of studying small populations could be fruitfully applied to study displacement of population caused by a big dam over a wide area. Another significant aspect about the study was the fact that Karve and Nimbkar had no intention to please the government by writing a success story; while they have also not said anywhere in the report that the dam was unnecessary. The results and the conclusions of the study simply revealed how the government, despite its stated good intentions for development, failed to deliver justice. In the foreword, the authors stated unequivocally:

> More dams have been built since independence than during the two hundred years of the British rule. . . With independence, this major activity became entirely a State sponsored enterprise. The State also realized that paying an adequate money compensation did not end the responsibility of the State and that people so displaced must be rehabilitated by the State.
>
> The following report will show that the State understood its responsibility and tried honestly to fulfil it, but still the attempt was largely fruitless because the rehabilitation was not properly planned (Karve & Nimbkar 1969: 1).

The book contains eight sections and three appendices which included the findings as well as detailed description of the methodology along with the questionnaire schedules. Under the section on findings, the authors analyzed a huge mass of quantitative and qualitative data on landlessness, caste composition, occupational changes, education, housing, compensation and the impact of displacement on the social and religious life of the affected population. In the concluding section, the authors succinctly observed the sufferings of the displaced population caused by the mega development project owing to lack of planning and foresight. I quote from the monograph:

> The chief failure of rehabilitation lies in the lack of planning. . . What actually happened is that people did have to move in a hurry, and the government puts the blame for this on the indecision of the people themselves . . . the valley people did not have a clear idea of what was going to happen . . . they handed large cash amounts to people who had never before handled money, and left them to their own devices. The result was that much of this money was spent in transportation expenses, instead of being utilized in constructing houses (ibid. 1969: 106).

Interestingly, Karve and Nimbkar finally narrated the short-sighted approach of the government, which was revealed when the government gave a cash dole of a few hundred rupees to the displaced persons just before the general election of the country apprehending that the dissatisfaction of the affected people might have been dissipated towards the government. Suffice it to say that Karve and Nimbkar could not accept this approach by the government to the resettled families (ibid. 108).

XIII

I would now narrate the case of a unique anthropologist in the nationalist tradition who worked in post-independent India, mainly at the Anthropological Survey of India. The reason that I devote a separate subsection for him is that he contributed to the two major subfields of anthropology (Physical Anthropology and Social-Cultural Anthropology) with equal competence and his interests finally converged towards policy-making aimed at uplifting the marginalized and underprivileged sections of the society. The name of the anthropologist is Pranab Ganguly (1929-2014) and he can be regarded as a biocultural anthropologist rather than a physical or sociocultural anthropologist. Like his predecessors, B.S. Guha, D.N. Majumdar, S.S. Sarkar, K.P. Chattopadhyay and Irawati Karve, Ganguly conducted intensive fieldwork to collect his data on the biological and cultural aspects of the communities he studied and viewed the problems of human adaptation from a holistic perspective to work out policies for the betterment of the populations. His papers in prestigious national and international peer-reviewed journals on religion, material culture, life-cycle rites and judicial system of the tribes in Andaman and Nicobar Islands published in 1961-3 did not receive comprehensive treatment by the social and cultural anthropologists in India. Ganguly's interest in the study of the Onges of Little Andaman took its final shape during the mid-seventies when he published a full-length paper titled, 'The Negritos of Little Andaman Island: A Primitive People Facing Extinction', in the *Indian Museum Bulletin* in 1975. This paper can be regarded as one of the finest works on policy anthropology. The paper covered almost every aspect of this small island tribe in the context of the global debate on the position of anthropologists regarding the study of endangered and disappearing populations. Ganguly made his position clear after narrating the differences between two schools of thought on the task of anthropologists. He quoted Sol Tax's 1971 editorial of *Current Anthropology* in which Tax observed a 'split' among the anthropologists on what should constitute the urgent task before them after the eighth International Congress of Anthropological and Ethnological Sciences (IUAES) held in 1968. Should the anthropologists give priority to study the last speaker of a disappearing community to build up their theory or should they accept change as an obvious outcome and invest their time towards their development? While studying the Onges Pranab Ganguly clearly stated his position in the following manner:

> The author feels that the two approaches are not mutually exclusive, but are complimentary to each other. The study of vanishing tribes does not prevent anthropologists from being interested in urgent problems of development and change in large societies; both types of research may be carried on simultaneously (Ganguly 1975: 8).

I will now describe how Ganguly made his attempt to combine the aforementioned approaches in his own way in the long article on Onge. Apart from the detailed and meticulous ethnography written in the classical Malinowskian style which also included the physical anthropology and demographic contours of the tribe, Ganguly described the society and culture of the Onges like a professional social anthropologist. He described the material culture, subsistence activities, kinship, marriage, family, rites of passage, political organisation and the religion in a systematic and comprehensive manner. The most important part of the paper however, is the section on the policy aspects around the major problem faced by the Onges, which was their decreasing numbers. Ganguly investigated the problem of the depopulation of the Onges from a demographic perspective by carefully taking into consideration the three rival hypotheses, which were (i) economic exploitation, (ii) assassination of the natives by the colonists, and (iii) introduction of new diseases against which the natives had no immunity. Ganguly was probably the first anthropologist who studied the Onges for a long period of time from a biosocial perspective and differed with the aforementioned hypotheses. The disagreement was based on his own observation and reading of the history of Little Andaman and he did not hesitate to state his policy recommendations towards the betterment of the tribe in a bold manner. In Ganguly's words:

> Ameliorative measures such as establishment of coconut plantations, introduction of horticulture, distribution of iron implements and other useful articles, carrying out routine health surveys and giving medical

relief, etc., though very useful and commendable, cannot prevent the decline of Onge population. These do not even touch the fringe of the real problem. Systematic investigations into the causes of Onge infertility and proper remedial measures against them are now urgently required (Ganguly 1975: 25-6).

Finally, Ganguly proposed the long-term measure that the Onges should be relocated in Rutland Island 31 miles north of Little Andaman where they once lived but which they left to get away from an epidemic several decades ago. The island was capable of supporting the Onge population with their traditional mode of subsistence and Ganguly suggested that they should be allowed to live there without any outside interference because it would be increasingly difficult for them to survive in Little Andaman owing to 'the rising demands of officials and workers for pork, fish, honey, fruits, etc.' the staple food of the Onges (ibid).

If we look at the works of Pranab Ganguly in a chronological order, we find that, during 1960-6, he contributed to physical and sociocultural anthropology by using methods of anthropometry, ethnography and linguistics with equal competence and that his interest towards the formulation of policies was also visible in his later work on the Onge, which I have just described in the previous paragraphs. During the mid-seventies, Ganguly turned his attention towards macro-level data on large samples and he also organized his thoughts around the bigger problems of human adaptation and evolution in an ecosystem framework, although he was not a dogmatic supporter of maintenance of stability. In this context the research of Ganguly, and this was his most remarkable one, was on the gradual decline in the average height (a negative secular trend) of members of some tribal and caste populations in India. With Anadi Pal, Ganguly first wrote a short paper in a volume published by the University of Calcutta in 1974. In this paper, the authors presented figures on the average height of 20 population groups (caste and tribes) measured by different authorities over an interval of at least 25 years and concluded that unlike many Western and Asian countries the studied Indian populations had become shorter since the late nineteenth and early twentieth centuries (Ganguly & Pal 1974c: 42-8). It was a remarkable finding. Ganguly pursued the work and made it global by publishing under his single authorship a whole chapter in a book edited by the famous anthropologist William Stini in a World Anthropology series volume by Mouton in 1979. Ganguly began this chapter by challenging the then scholarship in physical anthropology, which presumed that the progressive increase in stature was a universal phenomenon as it happened in many technologically advanced Western and non-Western populations. In this chapter, he demonstrated with the help of simple anthropometric data that in India three groups out of every four have become shorter in varying degrees in the course of one or two generations and it was not due to malnutrition or inbreeding but probably caused by a relaxation of natural selection against undersized individuals (Ganguly 1979: 315-37).

In another pioneering study for which he had won the prestigious Bertillon Medal of France (in 1973) on the variation in physique in north India in relation to urbanization and economic status, Ganguly was able to show with the help of carefully controlled experimental design (rare in Indian physical anthropology) the relationship between various somatometric measurements and observations (e.g. height, weight and skin colour) and some socioeconomic parameters. For example, he found that, among the Brahmin and Muslim populations of western Uttar Pradesh in north India, the well-to-do men are significantly taller and heavier and have absolutely broader hips and shoulders than the poor. The increases in different measurements observed in the well-to-do clearly reflected a general enlargement in the size of the body. In the circumferential measurements of limbs and torso, the differences between the economic classes were particularly pronounced. The well-to-do men had significantly larger heads, larger in both length and breadth dimensions, than the poor (Ganguly 1974a: 3-43). One should note here that Ganguly perceptively used the term 'class' and not 'caste', since his empirical findings revealed that class differentiation within a caste was more important to understand the human biological variation in India—a point little recognized by the social anthropologists. It may be interesting to recall here Ganguly's comment published in *Current Anthropology* on Joan P. Mencher's famous article, 'The Caste System Upside Down or the Not-So-Mysterious East' in 1974. I quote from Ganguly:

> From my field investigations in 12 districts of western Uttar Pradesh, I have gained the impression that the north Indian Brahmins are really no better off than the low-ranked agricultural castes of that area (Ganguly 1974b: 482).

The last remarkable work of Ganguly which I will discuss is a theoretical paper entitled, 'The Problem of Human Adaptation: An Overview', published in *Man in India* in 1977. This paper was delivered as the presidential address at the anthropology and archaeology section of the 64th Indian Science Congress in Bhubaneswar held in 1977. In this brilliant article, Ganguly viewed the major human problems of the modern world (e.g. malnutrition and inequality) from the perspective of adaptation. For him, adaptation should be considered in its broadest sense, which must include society and culture. Under a section in this paper titled, 'Socioeconomic Milieu', Ganguly after reviewing the literature exhaustively, including his own study on the Brahmin and Muslim groups of western Uttar Pradesh, commented:

> From the foregoing discussion it should be evident that the socioeconomic status effect manifests itself at every stage of life from birth to adulthood. The upper-class children have significantly bigger bodies than the lower-class children, and this difference persists to a remarkable degree in the final adult size. It may be argued that the genetic potential for growth of the Indian children, who suffer under the constraints of adverse socioeconomic environment remains to some extent unrealized (Ganguly 1977: 10).

But how did the poor adapt to this adverse socioeconomic deprivation? Ganguly's answer to this basic question can be found in the next section of the article titled 'Nutritional Stress':

> Adaption to malnutrition during critical stages of growth is likely to induce permanent reduction of body size which, in turn, will reduce the energy needs of the body. People having small body size will survive more easily on low-calorie diets and they will have some adaptive advantage in areas where scarcity conditions prevail (ibid.: 10-11).

At this juncture, one may ask a very legitimate question, which is, 'Did Ganguly view poverty as a kind of adaptation only?' I would say 'Yes, Ganguly looked at the unconscious strategies of survival of the poor but he also viewed the extremes of this'. Let us proceed further with him through this paper:

> It may be mentioned here that the survival of a population through diminution of body size and reduction of energy requirements is possible if only the nutritional deficiencies remain within tolerable limits. When the stress of malnutrition becomes very acute, the adaptive advantage of size reduction loses much of its significance and the population is threatened with the danger of extinction (ibid.: 14).

After this statement, Ganguly cited the case of the Juang population of Orissa and mentioned the findings of a biochemist, J.K. Roy, of the Anthropological Survey of India, who found that owing to severe malnutrition the Juang population had been decreasing for the last 25 years.

Ganguly's paper on adaptation is a full-blooded biocultural exercise on macro-level policymaking and I regard this Indian Science Congress address of 1977 as the true successor of the lectures delivered by his teachers, Tarak Chandra Das in 1941 and Sasanka Sekhar Sarkar in 1951, at the congress. This is because, like his predecessors, Pranab Ganguly was also seized with the major national problems and the role of anthropology and anthropologists in providing some solutions to these problems.

Pranab Ganguly as a professional anthropologist belonged to post-colonial India who practised intensive fieldwork and published in physical and sociocultural anthropology with equal competence—a rare quality among his contemporaries, which has almost vanished from the succeeding generations of anthropologists in India. Ganguly, however, was not a run-of-the-mill empirical anthropologist. His remarkable works on the progressive decline of stature among 60 endogamous population groups and the relationship of somatic variability with economic condition and urbanization demonstrated the ability to interpret a huge mass of empirical data within a theoretical framework which was basically biocultural in nature. Most importantly, it should be emphasized that Pranab Ganguly was not an ivory tower scholar, who only gathered knowledge. He made sincere attempts to apply his findings in formulating policies for the welfare and betterment of the underprivileged sections of the Indian population whether they were the endangered Onges of Little Andaman or the vast majority of the malnourished and stunted people of independent India.

XIV

Finally, I will narrate the story of Vinay Kumar Srivastava (1952-2020), who was another remarkable public anthropologist in the post-independence India who, unlike Ganguly, had a Ph.D. from a foreign university and degrees in both anthropology and sociology. Vinay spent most of his anthropological career in teaching, at the University of Delhi and joined the Anthropological Survey of India in 2017 as its director but had an untimely demise in December 2020.

Vinay's first article in *The Eastern Anthropologist* was published in 1990 and the title of the article was quite unconventional. It read as '"Practice of" and "Practice in" Anthropology' in which he distinguished between the colonial and post-colonial practices of anthropology in India. According to him, with the birth of the new nations in the post-colonial era, we needed a 'national anthropology', a 'national perspective in congruence with our historical arena and felt needs'. Let me quote Vinay:

We were expected to evolve 'our' perspective without recklessly borrowing from the West: the Western models were useful in their contexts, and any uncontestable reliance on them would be detrimental to the understanding of local social reality (Srivastava 1990: 311).

While championing the cause for a national anthropology, Vinay Srivastava was also aware of the emotional underpinnings of nationalism which, he thought, should be avoided and his major emphasis was to integrate anthropology on the basis of its real strength: (i) biocultural approach, and (ii) people-centric intensive and participatory fieldwork. For him, practice in anthropology meant 'field work is *with* people, and not *on* people' (italics by Vinay). I quote him again:

With every multi-faceted development plan, the practising anthropology advises to undertake multi-faceted evaluatory study. At each step, the community participation is assured; the people are fully involved in the process of 'practising in'. As each ethnography is a joint creation between the anthropologist and the people, so is every practice (ibid.: 319).

Vinay's sense of nationalism in anthropology could be discerned in his views, which he expressed quite forcefully on the occasion of the diamond jubilee symposium of *The Eastern Anthropologist* held in the year 2008 when he was the editor of the journal. He stated:

I think we have not yet transcended the syndrome of colonialism, or what I would call, 'foreignism'. In other words, we crave for a publication in a 'foreign' or to be precise, non-Indian, journal, even if it is lesser known, has pitiable or just in-house circulation, publishes articles mostly in a foreign language with a couple of them in English, and is of poor quality. . . We are victims of what I would call—the 'halo-effect', that is, whatever is published in a foreign journal is of high quality. We may be ethnocentric about our language, region, and religion but not about our journals (Srivastava 2008a: 149-50).

Vinay, of course, did publish his important research articles in 'foreign journals', like *Anthropos*, *Anthropology Today*, *Current Anthropology*, *The Cambridge Journal of Anthropology*, *China*

Report and *Dialectical Anthropology* in 1982-2013, but he also published his brilliant papers in prestigious and widely-circulated Indian journals, like *The Eastern Anthropologist*, *Man in India*, *Indian Anthropologist*, *Journal of Human Ecology*, *Journal of the Indian Anthropological Society* and *Economic and Political Weekly* throughout his academic career. Two of his most important papers were published in the *Economic and Political Weekly* in 1999 and 2008, respectively. Both the papers revealed Vinay's lifelong interest in public anthropology since he was not an ivory tower scholar studying kinship algebra or religious symbolism divorced from the political economy and the material existence of human life. But then he was not a business anthropologist who only judged anthropology by its market value. In his 1999 *EPW* article entitled 'The Future of Anthropology', Vinay argued that, in the context of the current trend in which the anthropologists only aspire for mere policy prescriptions and recommendations, a bright future could not be foretold for the discipline. In his words:

> A perilous consequence of this trend is that, instead of illuminating the functioning and dynamics of society and culture in particular and general terms, it confines itself to the question of policy prescription. By directing their energies to the 'issues of usefulness', anthropologists have come to think that the future survival of anthropology is incumbent upon its immediate market value. The future of anthropology can be enhanced, instead, by giving primacy to an interpretive understanding of societies and cultures, thereby making comments on existing policies for development and social justice more perceptive and relevant (Srivastava 1999: 545).

I now come to the 2008 *EPW* article, which reflected how Vinay practised anthropology when it came to policy. This article showed the 'practice in' that Vinay proposed in his earlier article on the future of anthropology. The article was titled as 'Concept of "Tribe" in the Draft National Tribal Policy'. It is important to note that, in this article, Vinay did not hesitate to subject both the draft national tribal policies under the National Democratic Alliance (NDA) and Union Progressive Alliance (UPA) governments to severe criticism. He was not also reluctant to show how the anthropological image of tribe as the earliest stage of social evolution sneaked into the governmental policy draft and resulted in the loss of tribal voice. I quote Vinay:

> Tribes have themselves done a lot for their own improvement—they have led movements for environmental protection, saving their cultural and human rights, throwing the exploiters out of their territories, regaining rights over their lost land and other resources, closing liquor shops in their area, curbing practices of conspicuous consumption, and putting a full stop to all those practices that reduce their respect in the eyes of others (Srivastava 2008: 35).

According to Vinay the much-vaunted governmental tribal policy draft, therefore, failed to earn the confidence of the tribals for whom it was prepared:

> This dynamic reality of tribal living is missing in the draft; what it lacks is the 'tribal voice'; what one hears is the discourse of the bureaucrats. Throughout the text runs the 'we-they' distinction; what *we* (the outsiders) think about what *they* (the tribes) want; and what *we* think tribes should be given. That is why the draft may not give confidence to the tribal people, notwithstanding its good intentions and suggestions (ibid. 35).

Six years later, Vinay continued his journey of public anthropology on the aforesaid tribal policy draft and reiterated his stand taken up in the 2008 *EPW* paper (rather softly) in an online monthly popular magazine named *One India One People*. His article published in 2014 was titled as 'Drafting the National Tribal Policy is Half the Work Done' and he again appealed that the 'draft policy is widely discussed' because the 'targeted beneficiaries wait ceaselessly for their lot to ameliorate' (Srivastava 2014). After joining the Anthropological Survey of India as director in March 2017, Vinay continued in his role as a public anthropologist by writing on the anthropological interests on Mahatma Gandhi (Srivastava 2019: 135-41) as well as on the 'Draft Policies for Great Andamanese and Sentinelese' (Srivastava et. al. 2020b: 165-76).

I would end my commentary on Vinay Kumar Srivastava as

a public anthropologist who made remarkable contributions not only to anthropological theory and methods but also on the question of how to bring in nationally relevant good practices by the anthropologists in India. Vinay's lifelong crusade against obscurantism, exclusion and stigma as vividly (ethnographically) expressed through his pioneering writings on sanitation in Delhi and the pandemic caused by Covid-19 are remarkable (Srivastava 2014: 275-90 & 2020a: 385-98). In this connection, let me bring in an article of Vinay Srivastava published in 2012 in *Social Change*. In this valuable article entitled 'Indian Anthropology Today', Vinay viewed anthropologists not simply as 'dispassionate observers' of social reality but also as 'conscientious citizen(s)', who expected all societies and States to be 'just, civil, and inclusive' (Srivastava 2012: 359). This is the message Vinay Kumar Srivastava left for us. Vinay's untimely demise in December 2020, however, prevented him to explore the factual results of the dialectics between these two roles of the Indian anthropologists in the context of nation-building, which I believe is a great loss to Indian anthropology.

NOTES

1. Srinivas seemed to be uninterested in the problems of famine, partition and displacement caused by industrialisation and installation of big dams in post-independent India, let alone the role of these important events on caste system and social change. We do not find any mention or reference to the aforementioned events in the 42 essays collected in *The Oxford India Srinivas* book published in 2009. For Srinivas, the 'non-violent revolution' in India, characterised by adult franchise, protective discrimination and land reforms, was entering a violent phase and he only ended with a generalized statement: 'The road to nation-building is a long and hard one especially when a country is as large, old, diverse and stratified as India' (Srinivas 2009: 387).
2. It may be noted that rehabilitation of displaced persons by the partition of the country occupied separate chapters in the first two

Planning Commission reports during 1951-6 and 1956-61. No such chapters were included in the subsequent reports of the Planning Commission of India. We do not find any special attention by the Planning Commission of India on the rehabilitation of persons affected by development caused displacement in its reports.

3. It should be noted here that pioneering Indian anthropologists unequivocally expressed their views on the role and importance of anthropology towards nation-building and national integration in a diverse country like India. D.N. Majumdar and B.S. Guha, in their articles published in 1947 and 1949, respectively, emphasised the potential role of anthropology not only in administration but also in combating the divisive forces inimical to nation-building. Guha, for example in his 1949 article on the progress of anthropology in India, stated: 'The importance of acquiring correct and adequate knowledge of the social and religious institutions of the people in a country of so diverse races and tribes is not only of scientific but also of utmost practical value in administration, as well as for ensuring fellowship and understanding among the population. Racial prejudice and communal animosities breed on ignorance and the surest method of stopping it is by appreciating each other's habits of life and modes of thought. Such knowledge leads to the development of harmony and a centrifugal outlook which is the great cementing force in a nation of many races (Guha 1949: 610-11).' We find a similar view in Verrier Elwin's article in *Man* on Anthropological Survey of India (see Elwin 1948: 68-9 & 80-1).
4. Here it would be relevant to note that K.S. Singh, who was the director general of the Anthropological Survey of India (1984-93), consistently studied famines in India in the post-independence period and wrote a book and a number of articles on famine. In one of his articles entitled, 'Human Response to Famine: An Anthropological Perspective', published in the *Human Science* in 1989, Singh noted that famines in India have a relationship with the rise of nationalist feelings and political awakening cutting across caste and religion leading to voluntary welfare measures by non-state organisations (Singh 1989: 267-73; see also Singh 1987-8: 186-205).
5. In this connection, I will mention an article by S.B. Chakrabarti published in the official journal (then named *Human Science*) of the Anthropological Survey of India in 1986, a year before the book by Kalla and Singh was published. The author in the article entitled 'Role of Human Sciences in National Development: A Critical

Appraisal' proposed 'an assertive stand on the role of human scientists in the development of a nation'. By seeking an 'assertive stand', the author criticized so called 'basic' and 'value free' research by the 'privileged elite in the corridor of big power', but he himself made little effort to discover the applied researches done by his predecessor anthropologists on famine, partition and development-caused displacement which affected millions of people in newly independent India (Chakrabarti 1986: 88-93).

6. Interestingly, in their edited book Kalla lamented: 'In spite of the notable usefulness of physical anthropology in India, with its given and much improvable standards, it has so far not found its due place in nation-building (Kalla 1987: 7).' He blamed some 'well-connected anthropologists' for practicing a 'cold war' against physical anthropology and the social anthropologists, in particular, for their domination in the national scene (ibid. 7-8).
7. Amitabha Basu was one of the most sensitive physical anthropologists in post-independence India who always looked for social purpose and relevance of anthropology in India (Basu 1974: 17-23; 2004: 1-20 & 2009: 290-306). In his 1974 article, Basu viewed the inner conflicts of the loyalty of a post-independence anthropologist being 'torn between two cultures: the culture of colonial anthropology in which the lifestyle and physique of remote people were studied for the esoteric pleasure of the standard-bearers of the colonial Raj or for the convenience of the colonial administration, and the culture of a new generation of unquiet youth whose sense of belonging to the wider social scene demands a pragmatic approach (Basu 1974: 17).'
8. T.C. Das' two articles published in the *Sociological Bulletin* dealt with unconventional and new topics of sociological research even by today's standards. In one article, Das described and analysed his empirical findings on the impact of industrialisation on the Hindu and Muslim populations in nine villages in the vicinity of Calcutta city (Das 1960: 46-59). The other paper was on the nature and extent of social change among the tribals of eastern India (Das 1962: 221-38).
9. The idea of improvement in agriculture in Bengal through the formation of co-operatives in the context of landlessness and small holdings is not a left luggage till today. In the West Bengal Human Development Report published by the government of West Bengal in 2004, we find under its chapter entitled, 'The Way Forward', a suggestion which reads as follows:

'The state government could consider new and imaginative ways of encouraging co-operatives in production and marketing in both agricultural and non-agricultural activities especially in rural areas (WBHDR 2004: 214).'

10. Surajit Sinha was a student of T.C. Das and received his training in social anthropological fieldwork from Das. Sinha noted in one of his articles:
'T.C. Das tried to rigorously develop field methods which could be fruitfully utilized in describing the living conditions of tribals, peasants as well as urbanites. He felt convinced that anthropological method of detailed contextual observation would be of immense help in social reconstruction (Sinha 1971: 7).'
11. Nirmal Kumar Bose in his article 'Problem of National Integration' had just mentioned B.S. Guha's survey on social tension among the Hindus and Muslims without further comments on its important findings and analyses (Bose 1962: 57).

CHAPTER 6

Conclusion

I

Unlike Western countries, research on the history of anthropology in India has not yet become a formidable tradition. There are few published works on the history and the development of anthropology in India, which included L.P. Vidyarthi's magnum opus entitled, *Rise of Anthropology in India: A Social Science Orientation* (vols. I & II). Vidyarthi, however, did not mention B.S. Guha's account of the history of Indian anthropology, which was published by the Indian Science Congress as early as 1938. In fact, Guha's article entitled 'Progress of Anthropology in India during the Past Twenty-Five Years' was the first comprehensive account on the history of Indian anthropology by an Indian anthropologist. Vidyarthi also could not find any substantial attempt to search for a nationalist trend of social and cultural anthropology in India. Interestingly, both D.N. Majumdar and B.S. Guha, in their articles on the progress of anthropology in India published in 1947 and 1949, respectively, emphasised the importance of anthropology as a holistic discipline in the task of building a new nation (Majumdar 1947: 1-31; Guha 1949: 607-13).

Existing works, though contained a lot of useful data on the history of anthropology during the colonial and post-colonial periods, did not venture into a search for the growth of nationalist anthropological writings by the Indian anthropologists or the role of the anthropologists in nation-building in the pre-and post-independence periods.

The standard critique of Indian anthropology as advanced by some of the Indian anthropologists viewed anthropology in post-independent India as a product of colonial tradition in which the Indian anthropologists, for various reasons followed their colonial masters in one way or the other. There also existed another view—that an Indian form of anthropology could be discerned in many ancient Indian texts and scriptures before the advent of a colonial anthropology introduced by the European scholars, administrators and missionaries in the Indian subcontinent.

In this broader context, it is argued that, while criticizing Indian anthropology, the critics mostly ignored the studies done by the pioneers of the discipline that were socially relevant and directed to the welfare and betterment of the underprivileged sections of our country.

Along with the colonial tradition, a nationalist trend in Indian anthropology could also be discerned which was growing during the pre- and post-independence periods in India and this trend was characterized by the works of the anthropologists who were socially committed and contributed to nation-building through their analytical writings and research. These anthropologists learned the methodology of the discipline from the West but did not become blind followers of Europe and America and they also did not want to derive their anthropology from the religious scriptures of the ancient Hindus. Instead, they visualized an Indian character of anthropology, which according to them, could be used in nation-building, a task which could not be developed into full maturity by their own successors.

The future of anthropology in India in the broader context of nation-building cannot be understood without looking into its past. The true nationalist tradition of anthropology in India, or for that matter in any country, cannot be developed without looking into the works of the anthropologists which contributed towards the task of nation-building. In more recent periods, the non-anthropologists (economists, historians and political scientists) who debated on the problems of nationalism and nation-building in India missed the contributions of anthropologists towards nation-building during the early years after independence. Therefore, I raised the question: Were there anthropological studies done to address some of the vital problems faced by the policymakers of independent India in the early years after independence of the country? In particular, did the anthropologists study (a) famine, (b) partition and resettlement of refugees, and (c) the socioeconomic impact of mega-industrialization and dam building? Undoubtedly, these three were among the major challenges which not only confronted post-independent India in its early years but continued for a long period of time. Five most important studies done by the anthropologists on the above challenges which confronted nation-building in its early phase have been described in this book. A summary of the features of these studies are now enumerated.

The first common feature of these anthropological studies was that, except the study done by T.C. Das on the Bengal famine, all of them were commissioned and sponsored either by the central or the state government of independent India which engaged anthropologists on matters related to displacement and resettlement. Das' study was funded partly in its later stage by the University of Calcutta. The second feature of these studies was that they were not specifically directed towards any particular ethnic minority or community, as had been in the case of anthropologists following the colonial tradition, but simply at the populations affected by partition and development processes. The third common denominator of these studies was their solid empirical database. In all these studies, the main objective of the authors was to collect, organize and analyze quantitative and qualitative data on the problem which they wanted to investigate. Fourth, the analyses of the data were also done not to test or generate any theory or hypothesis as regards the human populations, societies and cultures involved in the processes but to collect concrete factual materials on the ground realities of displacement of human populations in the newly independent nation. Fifth, in all the studies we find that the anthropologists innovatively employed their traditional methods (participant observation, genealogy, case study etc.) to large populations. Finally, these studies were done not for seeking pure knowledge but to generate policies around the major challenges encountered by the planners of the newly independent country in the post-colonial period. In short, these studies can be viewed as sincere attempts by the anthropologists towards the making of a new nation and that still remains outside the mainstream debates and discussion around nation-building by the social scientists and even by the anthropologists themselves. Under the changing times, the future of nationalist anthropology in India lies in carrying forward this remarkable tradition of anthropology developed by the pioneers.

II

Anthropology is an eclectic subject which developed into a professional discipline under the patronage of the British colonial government in India. The teaching of anthropology at Calcutta University began during the colonial period and, subsequently, anthropology departments in a number of universities in India were established after the independence of the country. The first Indian journal of anthropology, *Journal of the Anthropological Society of Bombay*, was founded in 1886 and the second, *Man in India*, started in 1921. The Anthropological Survey of India, the largest governmental organization of anthropology started its journey in 1945. Two major journals of anthropology, *The Eastern Anthropologist* and the *Bulletin of the Anthropological Survey of India*, began in 1947 and 1952, respectively. By and large, anthropology as an academic discipline enjoyed an institutional growth in the post-colonial period, which was not seen during the colonial period. Despite the immense potential of anthropology towards policymaking and application, policy research and advocacy in Indian anthropology have not yet become a well-developed tradition. In other words, despite the institutional support received by anthropology in the post-independence period, the anthropologists in India could not play an easily observable role towards nation-building by providing solutions for the major problems of the country. My research, however, showed that anthropologists did make attempts to study some of the major problems (viz., famine, rehabilitation of refugees and development-caused displacement) encountered by the country in the early periods of nation building, which I have described in detail in the previous chapters of this book. Under the changing times and circumstances, the future of nationalist anthropology in India lies in carrying forward this remarkable tradition of anthropology (as found in the works of the anthropologists like Pranab Ganguly and Vinay Srivastava) developed by the pioneers and this justified the historical exploration of nation-building in Indian anthropology beyond the colonial legacy.

Bibliography

Ahmed, A.S., *Defining Islamic Anthropology*, *RAIN*, 1984, p. 4.

Ambedkar, B.R. *The Untouchables: Who were they and why they became Untouchables?* New Delhi: Amrit Book Company, 1948.

——, *Castes in India: Their Mechanism, Genesis and Development*, paper presented at an anthropology seminar taught by Dr A.A. Goldenweizer at Columbia University, 1916, text first printed in: *Indian Antiquary*, vol. XLI, May 1917, reprinted as *Dr Babasaheb Ambedkar: Writings and Speeches*, vol. I., ed. Vasant Moon, Education Department, Government of Maharashtra, Mumbai, 1979.

——, 'Castes in India: Their Mechanism, Genesis and Development, in V. Moon (ed.) *Dr Babasaheb Ambedkar: Writings and Speeches*, vol. 1, Mumbai: Education Department, Government of Maharashtra, Mumbai, 1979.

Anthropological Survey of India, *Social Impact Assessment (A Module)*, Unpublished draft, Kolkata: Anthropological Survey of India, 2010.

Asad, T., ed., *Anthropology & the Colonial Encounter*, New York: Humanity Books, 1973.

Balakrishnan, V., Comment, pp. 4-5, in *Journal of the Indian Anthropological Society*, 15, 1-14 on the article by A. Basu, and S.K. Biswas, ('Is Indian Anthropology Dead/Dying?'), 1980.

Basu, A., 'An Anthropologist in Search of a Purpose: The Test-Case of the Pahira of Manbhum', *Indian Museum Bulletin*, 1974, pp. 17-23.

——, 'Human Biology in India: Its Possible Role in a Third World Society under Rapid Transformation', *Collegium Anthropologicum*, 1987, pp. 233-50.

——, 'Popularizing Anthropology: Do We Have Enough "Popular Eggs" in Our Basket?' in *Discourse on Development: Anthropological Dimension*, ed. R.K. Das and A. Guha, Midnapore: Department of Anthropology, Vidyasagar University, 2004, pp. 1-20.

——, 'An Anthropologist Looks at Anthropology in the Contemporary Social Scenario', in the *World of Dr B.M. Das: A Tribute*, ed. B. Choudhury and P.J. Mahanta, Guwahati: Assam Academy for Cultural Relations, 2009, pp. 290-306.

Basu, A. & S.K. Biswas, 'Is Indian Anthropology Dead/Dying?', *Journal of the Indian Anthropological Society*, 1980, pp. 1-14.

Bera, G., 'Development of Indian Anthropology', *Journal of the Indian Anthropological Society*, 1995, pp. 229-36.

Béteille, A., 'Introduction', in *Essays in Social Anthropology*, K.P. Chattopadhyay, Calcutta: K.P. Bagchi & Company, 1994.

——, 'Newness in Sociological Enquiry', *Sociological Bulletin*, 1997, pp. 97-110.

——, 'Teaching and Research', *Seminar*, November issue, 2000, pp. 20-3.

——, 'Ourselves and Others', *Annual Review of Anthropology*, 2013, pp. 1-16.

Bhattacharya, R.K., 'Holistic Approach to Anthropology: B.S. Guha's Vision of the Anthropological Survey of India', *Journal of the Anthropological Survey of India*, 2012-13, pp. 365-71.

Bhattacharya, D.K., 'From The Editor's Desk', *Indian Anthropologist*, 1991, pp. 1-4.

Bhattacharya, R.K. & J. Sarkar, *Anthropology of B.S. Guha (A Centenary Tribute)*, Calcutta: Anthropological Survey of India, 1996.

——, 'B.S. Guha: The Founder Director of the Anthropological Survey of India', in *Anthropology of B.S. Guha (A Centenary Tribute)*, ed. R.K. Bhattacharya, & J.K. Sarkar, Calcutta: Anthropological Survey of India, 1996, pp. 1-13.

Bhattacharya, S., 'Antinomies of Nationalism and Rabindranath Tagore', *Economic & Political Weekly*, 2016, pp. 39-45.

Bhowmick, P.K., 'Development of Anthropology', *The Eastern Anthropologist*, 1984, pp. 353-74.

Book Notices, 1964, 'Obituary of T.C. Das', *Sociological Bulletin, 13*(2), 88, Retrieved from https://journals.sagepub.com/doi/pdf/10.1177/003802291964020 7.

Bose, K. 'Panchanan Mitra', *Current Science*, 2006, p. 1439.

Bose, N.K., 'Current Research Projects in Indian Anthropology', *Man in India*, 1952, pp. 121-33.

—— [Edited with a foreword], *Peasant Life in India: A Study in Indian Unity and Diversity*, Delhi: Anthropological Survey of India (memoir no. 5), 1961.

——, *Cultural Anthropology and Other Essays*, Calcutta: Indian Associated Publishing Company, 1st published in 1929, 1953.

——, 'Caste in India', in *Cultural Anthropology and Other Essays*, ed. N.K. Bose, Calcutta: Indian Associated Publishing Company, 1st published in 1929, 1953, pp. 171-91.

——, 'Research in Indian Anthropology', *Man in India*, 1962a, pp. 175-80.

——, 'Problem of National Integration', *Bulletin of the Anthropological Survey of India*, 1962b, pp. 57-61.

——, 'Progress of Anthropology and Archaeology', in *Fifty Years of Science in India*, Calcutta: The Indian Science Congress Association, 1963.

——, 'Class and Caste', *Economic Weekly*, 1965, pp. 1337-40.

——, *Problems of National Integration*, Shimla: Indian Institute of Advanced Study, 1967.

——, *Problems of Indian Nationalism*, Bombay: Allied Publishers, 1969.

——, 'Anthropology after Fifty Years, in D. Sen (ed.), *Indian Anthropology Today*, Calcutta: Department of Anthropology, Calcutta University, 1974, pp. i-iv.

Bose, P., 'The Anthropologist as 'Scientist'? Nirmal Kumar Bose, in P. Uberoi, N.P. Sundar & S. Deshpande (eds.), *Anthropology in the East: Founders of Indian Sociology and Anthropology*, Ranikhet: Permanent Black, pp. 290-329.

Bose, S., 'Some Landmarks of Indian Anthropology', *Human Science*, 1986, pp. 74-6.

Bulletin of the Department of Anthropology, 'A Brief Survey of the Indian Anthropological Literature 1946-7', 1952, pp. 154-9.

——, 'A Brief Survey of the Indian Anthropological Literature 1948-50', 1952, pp. 113-19.

Bulletin of Yale University, Panchanan Mitra, series 37, no. 1, 1941, pp. 295-6.

Burman Roy, J.J., 'Tragedy of Culture in Indian Anthropology', *Mainstream*, vol. XLIX, no. 12, 12 March 2011.

Burman Roy, B.K., '*Social Processes in the Industrialization of Rourkela*, New Delhi: Office of the Registrar General, India, Ministry of Home Affairs, 1968.

——, 'My Anthropological Field Situation: A Lost Home or a Promised Horizon', in *Field Studies on the People of India: Methods and Perspectives*, ed. Surajit Sinha, Calcutta: The Indian Anthropological Society, 1978.

——, 'Professor K.P. Chattopadhyaya: A Scientist with Social Concern', in G. Chattopadhyaya (ed.), *Life and Times of an Indian Anthropologist K.P. Chattopadhyaya: A Collection of Seminar Papers*. Calcutta: The Asiatic Society, 2000, pp. 50-1.

Cernea, M.M., 'Social Integration and Population Displacement: The Contribution of Social Science', *International Social Science Journal*, 1995, pp. 91-112.

Cháirez-Garza, J., 'B.R. Ambedkar, Franz Boas and the Rejection of Racial Theories of Untouchability', *South Asia: Journal of South Asia Studies*, 2018, https://doi.org/10.1080/00856401.2018.1431855.

Chakladar, H.C., *'Fifty Years Ago' in Nil Durpan or The Indigo Planting Mirror* by Dinabandhu Mitra (translated from Bengali by a native), edited with an introduction by Sankar Sengupta, Calcutta: Indian Publications, 1972, pp. 187-205.

Chakrabarti, S.B., 'Role of Human Sciences in National Development: A Critical Appraisal', *Human Science*, 1986, pp. 88-93.

——, 'Prof. Surajit Chandra Sinha (1926-2000): A Great Scholar and a Teacher of Anthropology', *The Oriental Anthropologist*, 2002, pp. 189-95.

——, 'Anthropology of Surajit Chandra Sinha: A Brief Note', *Journal of the Indian Anthropological Society*, 2003, pp. 103-6.

'Chatterjee, P., 'Beyond the Nation or Within?', *Economic & Political Weekly*, 1997, pp. 30-4.

Chatterji, R., 'An Indian Anthropology? What Kind of Object Is It?', in *Asian Anthropology*, ed. Jan Van Breman, Eyal Ben, Ariand Syed Farid Alatas. London: Routledge, 2005.

Chattopadhyaya, D., *Lokayata: A Study of Ancient Indian Materialism*, New Delhi: People's Publishing House, 1959.

Chattopadhyay, G., 'A Critical Appreciation of Professor K.P. Chattopadhyay's Work on Education', in *Life and Times of an Indian Anthropologist: K.P. Chattopadhyay*, ed. G. Chattopadhyay, Calcutta: The Asiatic Society, 2000, pp. 1-7.

Chattopadhyay, K.P., 'Sari Border Changes', in *Study of Changes in Traditional Culture*, ed. K.P. Chattopadhyay, Calcutta: University of Calcutta, 1957.

Chaudhuri, B. 'Some Emerging Areas of Research in Anthropology in India', *Indian Anthropologist*, 45(1), 2015, pp. 1-14.

Chaudhuri, N.C., 'Professor K.P. Chattopadhyay: The Teacher and an Anthropoligist, in Life and Times of an Indian Anthropoligist: K.P. Chattopadhyay, ed. G. Chattopadhyay, Calcutta: The Asiatic Society, 2000, pp. 52-9.

Cochrane, G., 'Policy Studies and Anthropology', *Current Anthropology*, 1980, pp. 445-58.

Danda, A., 'Anthropology in Contemporary India', *Journal of the Indian Anthropological Society*, 2017, pp. 4-16.

Das, N.K., 'Indian Anthropology: A Plea for Pragmatic Appraisal', *Bangladesh e-Journal of Sociology*, 2018, pp. 11-29.

Das, T.C., 'Some Notes on the Economic and Agricultural Life of a Little-known Tribe on the Eastern Frontier of India', *Anthropos*, vol. 32, 1937, pp. 440-9.

Das, T.C., 'Cultural Anthropology in the Service of the Individual and the Nation', *Presidential Address Delivered in the Section of Anthropology in the Twenty-Eighth Indian Science Congress*, Benares, 1941.

——, 'Practical Steps Towards the Improvement of Museums in India, *The Calcutta Review*, November 1943, pp. 97-100.

——, *The Purums: An Old Kuki Tribe of Manipur*, Calcutta: Calcutta University, 1945.

——, *Bengal Famine (1943): As Revealed in a Survey of the Destitutes of Calcutta*, Calcutta: Calcutta University, 1949.

——, 'A Scheme for Tribal Welfare', *Journal of Social Research*, 1960, 3:2, pp. 93-112.

Dasgupta, A., *Displacement and Exile: The State-Refugee Relations in India*, New Delhi: Oxford University Press, 2016.

Dasgupta, P.K., 'Impact of Industrialization on Tribal Life', *Bulletin of the Anthropological Survey of India*, 1964, pp. 85-106.

——, 'Cultural Factors in Industrialization: A Case Study in Chittaranjan, West Bengal', *Journal of Social Research*, 1965, pp. 76-82.

Dasgupta, S., 'Recasting the Oraons and the 'Tribe' Sarat Chandra Roy's Anthropology', in P. Uberoi, N. Sundar, & S. Deshpande (eds.), *Anthropology in the East: Founders of Indian Sociology and Anthropology*, Ranikhet: Permanent Black, 2007, pp. 132-71.

Datta, B.N., 'Ethnological Notes on Some of the Castes of West Bengal', *Man in India*, 1935, pp. 196-224.

——, 'Races of India: A Critique of Reports of Indian Anthropology', *Anthropological Papers*, Calcutta: Calcutta University, 1935, pp. 165-248.

——, 'Origin and Development of Indian Social Polity', *Man in India*, 1942, pp. 12-63.

——, *Dialectics of Hindu Ritualism* (Part I), Calcutta: Gupta Press, 1950.

——, *Swami Vivekananda: Patriot-Prophet*, 1st published in 1954, 2nd revised edition, Calcutta: Nababharat Publishers, 1993.

——, *Hindu Law of Inheritance (An Anthropological Study)*, Calcutta: Nababharat Publishers, 1957.

——, *Swami Vivekananda* (in Bengali), Kolkata: Nababharat Publishers, 1961.

Datta-Majumder, 'Anthropology During the War', *American Anthropologist*, 1947, pp. 159-64.

Debnath, B., 'Crisis of Indian Anthropology', *Economic and Political Weekly*, 1999, pp. 3110- 14.

Deshpande, S., 'India, Anthropology', *The International Encyclopedia of Anthropology*, (DOI: 10.1002/9781118924396.wbiea2355), ed. Hilary Callan, John Wiley & Sons, Ltd., 2018, pp. 1-18.

Directory of Anthropologists in India, Pranab Ganguly, ed. A. Basu, M.P. Basu, A.K. Adhikary, Calcutta: Anthropological Survey of India, Government of India, 1981, pp. 110-11.

Dubey, M., 'The Nationalism Debate: Past and Present, *Indian Journal of Public Administration*, 2017, pp. 1-12.

Elwin, Verrier, 'The Anthropological Survey of India: Part I, History and Recent Development', *Man*, 1948, pp. 68-9.

——, 'The Anthropological Survey of India: Part II, The Five-Year Plan', *Man*, 1948, pp. 80-1.

Elwin, V., 'Notes on the Juang', *Man in India*, 1948, pp. 1-146.

Frontline, 2014, Obituary, 'Gerald Berreman Pioneer of Caste Studies', https://frontline.thehindu.com/other/obituary/pioneer-of-caste-studies/article5643042.ece (Accessed on 08.04.2022).

Gaikwad, S.M., 'Ambedkar and Indian Nationalism', *Economic & Political Weekly*, 1998, pp. 515-18.

Gaillard, G., *Routledge Dictionary of Anthropologists*, London: Routledge, 2004.

Ganguly, P., 'Variation in Physique in North India in Relation to Urbanization and Economic Status', in *Bulletins et Mémoires de la Société d'anthropologie de Paris*, XIII Série, Tome 1 Fascicule 1, 1974a, pp. 3-43.

——, 'Comment on J.P. Mencher', *Current Anthropology*, 1974b, pp. 482-3.

——, 'The Negritos of Little Andaman Islands: A Primitive People Facing Extinction', *Indian Museum Bulletin*, 1975, pp. 7-27.

——, 'The Problem of Human Adaption: An Overview', *Man in India*, 1977, pp. 1-22.

——, 'Progressive Decline in Stature in India: A Study of Sixty Population Groups', *Physiological and Morphological Adaption and Evolution*, ed., William A. Stini, The Hague: Mouton Publishers, 1979, pp. 315-37.

Ganguly, P. & A. Pal, 'Secular Trend in Stature in India', *Indian Anthropology Today*, ed. D. Sen. Calcutta: Department of Anthropology, Calcutta University, 1974c, pp. 42-8.

Ghosh, A. 'The Historical Anthropology of Surajit Sinha', *Journal of the Indian Anthropological Society*, 2003, pp. 111-15.

——, 'History of Anthropology in India', http://nsdl.niscair.res.in/jspui/bitstream/123456789/519/1/PDF%204.11HISTORY_OF_ANTHROPOLOGY_IN_INDIA01.pdf.

Ghosh, J.C., 'Hindu Anthropology', *Anthropological Papers (New Series)*, Calcutta University Press: University of Calcutta, 1938.

Ghurye, G.S., *Social Tensions in India*, Bombay: Popular Prakashan, 1969.

Ghurye, G.S., *Caste and Class in India*, Bombay: Popular Book Depot, 1957.

Greenough, P.R., *Prosperity and Misery in Modern Bengal: The Famine of 1943-4*, New York: Oxford University Press, 1982.

Guha , A., 'Bengal Famine and a Forgotten Author', *Frontier*, 2010, pp. 90-4.

——, 'Tarak Chandra Das: A Marginalised Anthropologist', *Sociological Bulletin*, 2011, pp. 245-65.

——, 'T.C. Das Sitting in the Armchair: The Other Side of the Fieldworker Anthropologist', *South Asian Anthropologist*, 2016, pp. 109-114.

——, *Tarak Chandra Das: An Unsung Hero of Indian Anthropology*, (Foreword by Hari Mohan Mathur), Delhi: Studera Press, 2016a.

——, 'Unsung Anthropologists: Indian Anthropology and Its Critics', *Frontier*, 2016b, pp. 12-13.

——, 'Understanding Caste by B.R. Ambedkar and Nirmal Kumar Bose: A Comparison', Invited lecture delivered on 14 December 2016 in a National Conference on *Caste, Culture, Power: Indian Society* held during 14-16 December 2016 at the Anthropological Survey of India, North West Regional Centre, Dehradun, on the occasion of the 125th birth anniversary of Dr. B. R. Ambedkar, 2016c.

——,'Manuwadi Bias in Indian Anthropology', *Forward Press*, 28 September 2016d.

——, 'The Forgotten Thesis I & II', *The Statesman*, 9, 10 January 2017a, p. 8.

——, 'The Empire, Its Law and the Bankruptcy of Anthropologists', *Economic and Political Weekly*, 2017b, pp. 23-5.

——, 'In Search of Nationalist Trends in Indian Anthropology: Opening a New Discourse', *Occasional Paper No. 62*, Kolkata: Institute of Development Studies, 2018, pp. 3-41.

——, 'Nationalist Anthropology', *The Statesman*, 24 February 2018, p. 8.

——, 'Scrutinising the Hindu Method of Tribal Absorption', *Economic and Political Weekly*, 2018a, pp. 105-10.

——, 'Social Anthropology of B.S. Guha: An Exploration', *Indian Anthropologist*, 2018b, pp. 1-12.

——, 'Ambedkar and N.K. Bose on Caste', *Frontier*, 2018c, pp. 36-40.

——, 'Colonial Legacy and Hindu Anthropology', *Frontier*, 2019, pp. 81-3.

——, 'Bhupendranath Datta: An Unnoticed Indian Anthropologist', *Bulletin of the Ramakrishna Mission Institute of Culture*, LXX, 2019, pp. 20-3.

——, 'Colonial, Hindu and Nationalist Anthropology in India', *Sociological Bulletin*, 2019a, pp. 154-68.

——, 'A Forgotten Book by a Marginalised Anthropologist', *Social Change*, 2019b, pp. 493-506.

——, 'Nation Building on the Margins: How the Anthropologists of India Contributed?' *Sociological Bulletin*, 2021, pp. 59-75.

Guha, B.S., 'Dr. Panchanan Mitra', *Current Science*, 1936, p. 98.

——, 'Progress of Anthropology in India during the past twenty-five years', Calcutta: The Indian Science Congress Association, 1938.

——, 'Progress of Anthropological Research in India', *Anthropos*, 1946-9, pp. 607-13.

——, 'The Role of Social Sciences in Nation Building', *Sociological Bulletin*, 1958, pp. 148-51.

——, *Social Tensions among the Refugees from Eastern Pakistan*, Calcutta: Government of India, 1959.

Hutton, J.H., 'Obituary of K.P. Chattopadhyay', *Man*, 1963, pp. 155-6.

Jenkins, L. D., 'Another People of India Project: Colonial and National Anthropology', *Journal of Asian Studies*, 2003, pp. 1143-70.

Joshi, P.C., Personal communication over email dated 12 August 2019.

——, 'Advent of Anthropology and Birth of Social Anthropology in Delhi University', *The Eastern Anthropologist*, 2015, pp.35-41.

——, *Journal of the Indian Anthropological Institute*, Obituary of Ramaprasad Chanda, 1938, pp. i-iii.

Kalla, A.K. & K.S. Singh, 'Preface', in A.K. Kalla & K.S. Singh (eds.), *Anthropology Development and Nation Building*, New Delhi: Concept Publishing Company, 1987, pp. v-vi.

Kalla, A.K., 'Physical Anthropology: Its Relevance in Nation Building', in *Anthropology Development and Nation Building*, ed. A.K. Kalla & K.S. Singh, New Delhi: Concept Publishing Company, 1987, pp. 1-12.

Karve, Irawati and Jai Nimbkar, *A Survey of the People Displaced through the Koyna Dam*. Poona: Deccan College, 1969.

Kshitish Prasad Chattopadhyay (1897-1963), 'Notes and News', *International Journal of Comparative Sociology*, 1964, pp. 111-12.

Krishnamurty, J., 'Ambedkar's Educational Odyssey 1913-1927', *Journal of Social Inclusion Studies*, 2019, 5(2), pp. 147-57.

Kumar, A. , 'B.R. Ambedkar on Caste and Land Relations in India', *Review of Agrarian Studies*, 2020, pp. 37-56.

Kumar, V., 'How Egalitarian Is Indian Sociology?', *Economic and Political Weekly*, 2017, pp. 33-9.

Madan, T.N., 'Ramkrishna Mukherjee: In Memorium', *Economic and Political Weekly*, 2016, pp. 26-9.

Mahalanobis, P.C., R. Mukherjea, and A. Ghosh, 'A Sample Survey of After-Effects of the Bengal Famine of 1943', *Sankhyâ: The Indian Journal of Statistics*, 1946, pp. 337-400.

Majumdar, D.N., 'Progress of Anthropology in India (1911-46): A Brief Review', Delhi: The Indian Science Congress Association & The Council of Scientific and Industrial Research, 1947.

Majumder, P.P., 'Comment', in *Journal of the Indian Anthropological Society*, on the article by A. Basu, and S.K. Biswas (1980), 'Is Indian Anthropology Dead/Dying?, 1980.

Mehta, S., 'From Exotic to Empiric: Temptations and Turbulence in Contemporary Anthropology', *Indian Anthropologist*, 2002, pp. 25-46.

Mencher, J.P., 'The Caste System Upside Down or the Not-So-Mysterious East', *Current Anthropology*, 1974, pp. 469-93.

Misra, P.K. 'Anthropological Thoughts and Methdological Innovations of Surajit Chandra Sinha', *Journal of the Indian Anthropological Society*, 2003, pp. 139-57.

Mitra, S.C., 'A Plea for Nature Study in Indian Schools', *The Calcutta Review*, 1911, pp. 48-64.

Mitra, P., 'Research Leads in Anthropology in India, *Man in India*, 1933, pp. 1-16.

Mukherjee, D.P., 'Some Anthropological Contributions of Biraja Sankar Guha: A Study in Retrospect', *Anthropology of B.S. Guha (A centenary Tribute)*, ed. R.K. Bhattacharya and J.K. Sarkar, Calcutta: Anthropological Survey of India, pp. 35-82.

Mukherjee, R., C.R. Rao and J.C. Trevor, 'The Physical Characteristics of the Ancient Inhabitants of Jebel Moya, Sudan', Cambridge: Cambridge University Press, 1955.

——, 'Family Planning in Social and Economic Development: Some Points for Discussion', *Demography India*, 1973, pp. 121-30.

Mukhopadhyay, R., 'Dr. Bhupendranath Datta: Remembering a Great Scholar in Indian Anthropology and Sociology', *Journal of the Indian Anthropological Society*, 54, 2019, pp. 65-73.

——, 'K.P. Chattopadhyay and the Study of Kinship', in G. Chattopadhyay (ed.) *Life and Times of an Indian Anthropologist, K.P. Chattopadhyay: A Collection of Seminar Papers*, Calcutta: The Asiatic Society, 2000, pp. 39-49.

Munshi, S., 'Tribal Absorption and Sanskritisation in Hindu Society',*Contributions to Indian Sociology (NS), 1979*, 1979, pp. 293-317.

Nandy, A., 'Nationalism: Genuine and Spurious', *Economic & Political Weekly*, 2006, pp. 3500-4.

Nature, 'Dr. Panchanan Mitra', 31 October 1936, p. 750.

Negi, R.S., 'The 7th Nirmal Kumar Bose Memorial Lecture', New Delhi: Indira Gandhi National Centre for the Arts, 2013, pp.1-11.

Nehru, J., *The Discovery of India*, New Delhi: Oxford University Press, 1946.

Newsletter, vol. 2, no. 1 (March-April), Calcutta: Anthropological Survey of India, 1973.

Padmanabha, P. 'Indian Census and Anthropological Investigations', Paper presented in the Xth International Congress of Anthropological and Ethnological Sciences in Delhi, 1978, pp. 1-26. (http://www.censusindia.gov.in/data_products/library/anthropologic_link/anthro.pdf accessed on 9 November 2021).

Pakrasi, K., 'Occupation Class, Migration and Family Structure among the Refugees of West Bengal, 1947-8', *Man in India*, 1967, pp. 200-13.

Palit, C. & S. Sengupta, eds., *Navigating Nationalism*. Kolkata: Avenel Press, 2016.

Pathy, J., 'Imperialism, Anthropology and the Third World', *Economic and Political Weekly*, 1981, pp. 623-7.

Pandey, G., 'Questions of Nationalism and Communalism', *Economic & Political Weekly*, pp. 983-4.

Pellissery, S., 'Anthropology's Contributions to Public Policy: Introduction to Special Issue', *Indian Anthropologist*, 2014, pp. 1-20.

Piplai, D., 'Comment', in *Journal of the Indian Anthropological Society*, on the article by A. Basu, and S.K. Biswas, 'Is Indian Anthropology Dead/Dying?', 1980, pp.11-12.

Rakshit, H.K., ed., *Anthropology in India: vol. 2: Physical Anthropology*. Calcutta: Anthropological Survey of India, 1976.

Rao, P.V., 'The Future of Anthropology in India: A Reflection and a Perspective', *The Eastern Anthropologist*, 2012, pp. 205-20.

Ratnam, B., *Anthropology on the March*, Madras: The Book Centre, 1963.

Ray, S.K., *Bibliographies of Eminent Indian Anthropologists* (with Life Sketches), Anthropological Survey of India, Government of India, Indian Museum, Calcutta, 1974.

Raychaudhuri, T.C., 'Obituary of H.C.Chaklladar', *Man in India*, 1958, pp.138-139.

Roy, Sarat Chandra, 'An Indian Outlook on Anthropology', *Man*, 1938, pp. 146-50.

Sachchidananda, 'Planning, Development and Applied Anthropology in India, *Indian Anthropology*, 1973, 3(1): 1-16.

Sahay, B.N. 'Approach to Tribal Welfare in Past Independence Era', *Indian Anthropologist*, 1998, 28(1): 73-81.

Sahay, K.N., 'Teaching of Anthropology in India', *Indian Anthropologist*, 1976, pp. 1-19.

Sarana, G., and D.P. Sinha, 'Status of Social-Cultural Anthropology in India', *Annual Review of Anthropology*, 1976, pp. 209-25.

Sarkar, J., 'State of Cultural Anthropological Research in the Anthropological Survey of India', *Journal of the Anthropological Survey of India*, 2003, pp. 73-85.

——, 'The Jarwa Destine: A Critical Appraisal of Some Recommendations, *Journal of the Indian Anthropological Society*, 2003, pp. 167-72.

Sarkar, S.S., 'The Place of Human Biology in Anthropology and its Utility in the Service of the Nation', *Man in India*, 1951, pp. 1-22.

Sarkar, T., 'Birth of a Goddess', 'Vande Mataram', *Anandamath*, and Hindu Nationhood', *Economic & Political Weekly*, 2006, pp. 3959-69.

Sarana, G., 'The Study of Nation Building Process', in D. Sen (ed.), *Indian Anthropology Today*, Calcutta: The University of Calcutta, 1974.

Saraswati, B., 'Professor Nirmal Kumar Bose: The Gandhian Anthropologist', in T. Sen (ed.), *Nirmal Kumar Bose: Life, Works and Vision*, Kolkata: The Asiatic Society, 2003.

Sen, A., *Poverty and Famines: An Essay on Entitlement and Deprivation*, Oxford: Oxford University Press, 1999.

——, 'Is Nationalism a Boon or a Curse?' *Economic & Political Weekly*, 2008, pp. 39-44.

Sen Gupta, S., *Folklorists of Bengal*, Calcutta: Indian Publications, 1965.

Sengupta, S., (ed.), *Architects of Anthropology in India*, New Delhi: Gyan Publishing House, 2021.

Shah, A.M., 'Anthropology in Bombay, 1886-1936', *Sociological Bulletin*, 2014, pp. 355-67.

Shore, Cris, N. and S. Wright, 'Policy: A New Field of Anthropology', in Cris Shore and Susan Wright (eds.), *Anthropology of Policy: Critical Perspectives on Governance and Power*, London: Routledge, 1997, pp. 3-30.

Singh, K.S., 'Indian Anthropology 2000 AD: Problems and Prospects', *Human Science*, 1987, pp. 217-19.

——, 'Famine Nationalism and Social Change: The Indian Scenario', *Indian Historical Review*, 1987-8, pp. 186-205.

——, 'Human Response to Famine: An Anthropological Perspective', *Human Science*, 1989, pp. 267-73.

——, (ed.), *The History of the Anthropological Survey of India*, Calcutta: Anthropological Survey of India, 1991.

——, 'A Perspective on the ASI', *Seminar*, November 2000, (http://www.india-seminar.com/2000/495.htm.

Sinha, A.C., 'Indian Social Anthropology and Its Cambridge Connections', *The Eastern Anthropologist*, 1991, pp. 345-54.

——, 'Understanding Colonial Subjects', in Himanshu Roy, Jawaid Alam (eds.), *A History of Colonial India 1757 to 1947*, London: Routledge, 2021, pp. 76-91.

Sinha, D.P., & C.S. Coon, 'Biraja Sankar Guha, 1894-1961', *American Anthropologist*, 1963, pp. 382-7.

Sinha, S., *Resettlement of East Pakistan Refugees in Andaman Islands*, Alipore: Government of West Bengal, 1955.

——, 'Involvement in Social Change: A Plea for Own Ideas', *Economic and Political Weekly*, 1967, pp. 1707-9.

——, 'Urgent Problems for Research in Social and Cultural Anthropology in India: Perspective and Suggestions', *Sociological Bulletin*, 1968, pp. 123-31.

——, 'Is there an Indian Tradition in Social/Cultural Anthropology: Retrospect and Prospect?', *Journal of the Indian Anthropological Society*, 1971, pp. 1-14.

——, 'Foreword', in *Bibliographies of Eminent Indian Anthropologists (with Life-Sketches)*, Shyamal Kumar Ray, Anthropological Survey of India, Government of India, Indian Museum, Calcutta, 1974.

——, 'India: A Western apprentice', in *Anthropology: Ancestors and Heir*, ed. Stanley Diamond, The Hague: Mouton, 1980.

Sinha, S., 'Preface', in *Field Studies on the People of India: Methods and*

Perspectives, (ed.) Surajit Sinha. Calcutta: The Indian Anthropological Society, 1978.

——, Editorial of *Man in India*, 1985, pp. i-v.

——, 'The 1st Nirmal Kumar Bose Memorial Lecture', 1993, New Delhi: Indira Gandhi National Centre for the Arts, 1997, pp. 5-26.

Sinha, S.C., (ed.), *Anthropology in India: vol. 1: Cultural Anthropology*, Calcutta: Anthropological Survey of India, 1976.

Sinha, V., 'Indigenizing Anthropology in India', in *Asian Anthropology*, ed. by Jan Van Breman, Eyal Ben-Ariand Syed Farid Alatas, London: Routledge. 2005.

Srinivas, M.N., 'On Living in a Revolution', in *The Oxford India Srinivas*, first published in 1986, New Delhi: Oxford University Press, 2009, pp.373-87.

Srinivas, M.N. & M.N. Panini, 'The Development of Sociology and Social Anthropology in India', *Sociological Bulletin*, 1973, pp. 179-215.

Srivatsan, R., 'Native Noses and Nationalist Zoos', *Economic and Political Weekly*, 1986-1999.

Srivastava,V.K., '"Practice of" and "Practice in" Anthropology', *The Eastern Anthropologist*, 1990, pp. 301-23.

——, 'The Future of Anthropology', *Economic and Political Weekly*, 1999, pp. 545-52.

——, 'Teaching Anthropology', *Seminar*, 2000, pp. 33-9.

——, 'Some Responses of Communities to Social Tensions in India, *Anthropos*, 2003, pp. 157-65.

——, 'Concept of "Tribe" in the Draft National Tribal Policy', *Economic and Political Weekly*, 2008, pp. 29-35.

——, 'Indian Anthropology Today', *Social Change*, 42(3): 359-73, 2012 .

——, 'On Sanitation: A Memory Anthropology', *Social Change*, 2014, 44(2): 275-90.

——, 'Editorial' *Journal of the Anthropological Survey of India*, 2019, 68(2): 135-41.

——, 'Anatomy of Stigma: Understanding COVID-19', *Social Change*, 2020a, 50(3): 385-98.

——, 'Drafting the National Tribal Policy is Half the Work Done', 2014, *One India One People*, (http://oneindiaonepeople.com/drafting-the-national-tribal-policy-is-half-the-work-done/ accessed on 8 January 2021.

Srivastava, V.K., U. Kumar, M. Sasikumar, V.N. Pulamaghatta, S.K. Patel and P.A. Goyal, 'Draft of the Polices for Great Andamanese and Sentinelese, *Journal of the Anthropological Survey of India*, 2020b 69(1): 165-76.

Steward, J.H., 'Ecological Aspects of Southwestern Society', *Anthropos*, vol. 32, 1937, pp. 87:104.

Sundar, N., 'In the Cause of Anthropology: Life and Works of Irawati Karve', in P. Uberoi, N. Sundar, & S. Deshpande (eds.), *Anthropology in the East: Founders of Indian Sociology and Anthropology*, Ranikhet: Permanent Black, 2010, pp. 360-416.

Tauger, M., 'The Indian Famine Crises of World War II', *British Scholar*, 2009, pp. 166-96.

Uberoi, P., N. Sundar, & S. Deshpande, 'Indian Anthropology and Sociology: Towards a History', *Economic and Political Weekly*, 2000, pp. 1998-2002.

——, 'Introduction: The Professionalisation of Indian Anthropology and Sociology—People, Places and Institutions', P. Uberoi, N. Sundar & S. Deshpande (ed.), *Anthropology in the East: Founders of Indian Sociology and Anthropology* Ranikhet: Permanent Black, 2007, pp. 1-63.

University Grants Commission, *Model Curriculum Development Report in Anthropology*, New Delhi: University Grants Commission, 2001.

Vidyarthi, L.P., 'Problems and Prospects of Tribal Development in India', *Indian Anthropologist*, 1972, 2(2): 80-93.

——, *Rise of Anthropology in India: A Social Science Orientation*, vols. I & II., New Delhi: Concept Publishing Company, 1978.

Index